I0458942

See Through

*The Art and Cost of Radical Transparency
in a World That Profits from Pretending*

Stephanie M. Hutchins, PhD

For speaking engagements, permissions, or media inquiries, contact: info@serotinouslife.com

ISBN: 978-1-969823-01-5

Dedication

For the ones who've been told they're too much.

For the ones who've kept the peace at the cost of their truth.

For the ones who've been asked to perform, please, or prove themselves to be worthy of love, safety, or respect.

For the ones who risk speaking up—even when silence is safer.

This is for you.

May you never again feel like you have to bleed to be believed.

May you come home to yourself—unhidden, unarmored, and free.

Table of Contents

A Glimpse

It was supposed to be a normal day. The children were laughing. I was not. I sat cross-legged on the classroom floor in Vietnam, exhausted, raw, and unraveling. Something cracked open that day. Not a breakdown—a *breakthrough*. I had nothing left to prove and nowhere left to hide. That was the day I stopped performing and started listening.

This isn't a story of collapse. It's a story of clarity—of finally listening to the parts I once silenced just to make it through.

Author's Note

Dear Reader,

I've spent most of my life circling the truth—sometimes rushing to share it before I was ready, other times keeping it hidden beneath perfectionism, fear, or the pressure to be palatable. Either way, I was searching for something real, not performance. The kind of honesty that lets you breathe deeper inside your own skin.

This is the book I wasn't sure I'd ever write. Not because I lacked the words, but because I finally learned to protect them. For years, I believed that being real meant being transparent about everything—especially the painful parts. I opened myself wide in books, classrooms, and late-night messages, not to be provocative, but to prove I understood what hurt. That vulnerability—the state of openness—helped people, sometimes profoundly. But I hadn't yet understood that transparency is different: it's the conscious choice to share that openness. Without grounding, either can become a slow erosion—of clarity, of boundaries, of self.

So this book isn't about hiding. It's about discernment—telling the truth without handing yourself over, being honest without collapsing just to be believed. True respect doesn't come from unraveling, from making pain into spectacle, or from proving your worth through suffering. It comes from transparency guided by discernment and rooted in self-trust.

Even now, a voice still rises sometimes: Who do you think you are—to write a memoir, to take up this kind of space? But I know that voice. It's not truth. It's an echo—of small-town silence, early wounds, and long histories of being told I was too much and would never be enough. So no, this isn't arrogance. This is alignment.

I've lived, healed, and reclaimed my voice more times than I can count. That's what gives this story its power—not polish, not perfection, but persistence. This isn't a story of being exceptional. It's a story of being authentic. And if you've ever wondered whether your story matters—even if you're still finding the words for it—I hope this book reminds you: *you and your story matter.*

This story is personal, yes—but it's also deeply collective. The patterns we unravel in ourselves often echo the ones that exist in our families, our communities, and our workplaces. What we unlearn privately can create ripple effects publicly. Whether you're reading this alone or in a group, I hope this book offers not just a mirror, but a conversation. One that makes more room for truth in your own life, and in the spaces that shape it.

With love and deep admiration,
Stephanie

Choosing to Be Seen

You already know what it feels like to disappear—not all at once, but in pieces: a softened voice here, a swallowed truth there, a smile offered when you wanted to scream. You've lived the cost of staying palatable in rooms that never learned to hold your fullness. You might have called it strength or survival—even convinced yourself that safety meant shrinking, making yourself smaller to avoid the blow, even as another part of you overcompensated by becoming the loudest voice in the room.

By the time I sat down to write this, I had reached a threshold; I could no longer tell my story in ways that cost me more than they gave. *See Through* begins there: not in display, but in quiet conviction. I didn't write this book to be shocking. I wrote it because disappearing—emotionally, spiritually, energetically—was no longer an option. I had carried the pressure to be inspiring, useful, and honest in ways that drained me more than I could name. And still, I chose to tell the truth—not all at once, but clearly, intentionally, without apology.

This isn't just a book I decided to write. It's the one that kept finding me, until I finally let it lead.

And I'm still learning. I don't have it all figured out—not healing, not boundaries, not how to stay soft in a world that rewards sharpness. I'm writing this from the middle of the work, not the end. And that's part of the message. In classrooms, coaching sessions, and late-night conversations with friends and family, I've seen the same truths surface repeatedly: the longing to be seen without being split apart, the desire to be trusted without having to relive every wound. Those moments have shown me that what I've lived is not just personal—it's part of a wider pattern, and one worth speaking to.

Living *see through* isn't easy. Especially when the world asks us to stay small, stay smiling, stay silent. But I'd rather be honest than polished. I'd rather be in-process than pretending.

There came a point when telling the truth no longer felt freeing. I hadn't learned the difference between speaking to be witnessed and speaking from what I could hold. Sometimes it healed me; other times it left me depleted and unsure of who I was outside of the telling. It didn't arrive all at once. The reckoning came slowly, asking me to stop broadcasting and start listening—to myself first.

See Through began as a turning point; the slow, often painful process of facing the truths I once hid behind polished narratives and exaggerated healing. But it didn't stay there. It became something bigger: an offering. A reflection. A companion for those still wondering if it's safe to be real.

If you've ever felt like the world only welcomes you in pieces—the quiet parts, the pretty parts, the palatable parts—this book is for you. Not because I have all the answers, but because I've carried the same ache: to be seen fully without having to fracture in the process.

At its core, *See Through* is about living transparently without losing yourself—where vulnerability is the felt openness, transparency is the choice to share it, and sovereignty is the self-trust that decides when and how. It's truth-telling that doesn't demand self-erasure, boundary-setting without apology, and reclaiming your voice without having to relive your worst moments to be heard. It's part memoir, part mirror—a personal homecoming that invites your own.

I wrote this book now because I reached a crossroads. I could no longer hold space for everyone else's healing while avoiding the parts of mine that needed deeper integration. And I know I'm not the only one. We live in a moment that praises openness and punishes truth. Exposure is rewarded; boundaries cost you. The result is familiar: emptied out, still unseen. *See Through* is my answer to that tension—a map for coming home to yourself on your own terms.

See Through didn't begin in Vietnam, but that's where I realized it had to be next. I started formulating it nearly a year earlier, in the thick of dismantling some of the deepest beliefs that had quietly blocked my biggest goals. At the time, I thought my fourth book would align with a new academic coaching business I was building—polished, strategic, and safe.

But during a month of volunteer work in Vietnam—a project I entered with the intention to give—I came face-to-face with the ways I'd been overgiving for years. I wasn't just helping. I was splintering. Not visibly, but energetically; bending to accommodate, abandoning myself in the name of impact.

The ceiling fan hummed overhead. Outside, motorbikes threaded the streets like a steady undercurrent. In the press of those long, heavy days, I made a quiet decision: postpone the business, shelve the "smart" book, and let *See Through* take its place. Not because the other work didn't matter, but because this one wouldn't wait.

That choice in the heat of Vietnam became the foundation for every chapter that followed—because this book is built on the quiet, decisive moments when we stop abandoning ourselves. Every story in these pages carries the same current: a rhythm of letting go, reclaiming, and beginning again.

The heat lingered that week—thick, unrelenting, asking me to slow down and notice what I was carrying. Out of that heaviness came a different kind of clarity—the kind that shifts small choices first. A few days later, I muted a conversation with someone I truly cared about. Not out of spite, but to protect the peace I'd spent a decade learning to hold. That moment wasn't about drama. It was about clarity. I didn't owe an explanation. I owed myself consistency.

This is what the book is about: quiet shifts, hard boundaries, small pivots that signal something far more sacred—a soul returning to itself.

I've spent years helping others tell their stories—in coaching rooms, classrooms, and late-night messages where truth felt safer than pretense. I've sat across from people unraveling their own histories, and I've held space for their voices to rise. But *See Through* is the first time I've fully turned that mirror on myself—not as a gesture of confession, and certainly not to shock anyone. This isn't about putting my pain on display. It's choosing honesty over self-erasure.

Before this, I wrote three books. Each one came from a raw, vulnerable place—and I don't regret a word. Those pages helped people feel recognized. They let others know they weren't alone. And I'm proud of the version of me who wrote them. She told the truth with the tools she had. She shared everything, even the parts still forming, because she believed that openness could heal—and often, it did.

But I've since learned that healing for others can come at a cost to yourself if the timing isn't right. I hadn't yet understood what happens when you offer too much, too soon—before you've had a chance to hold it with care. Telling your story before you've learned to carry it gently can leave you threadbare.

4

I learned this the hard way during webinars where I'd invite guests to stay afterward for questions. I was grateful for their vulnerability, but in my eagerness to show how much I understood their suffering, I would step back into my own. I'd relive it just long enough to meet them where they were—and then spend hours that night, and the nights after each webinar, lying awake with my nervous system on high alert. Eventually, I began to dread those closing moments, knowing I'd have to walk back through my pain again. It made me a less present teacher the next day and a thinner version of myself at home.

The guests often thanked me profusely, especially those who stayed late. But I had paid too high a price to keep proving I understood. There's a tenderness that gets lost when you give everything away too early—not because your truth isn't valid, but because your nervous system isn't ready for what comes next. I've since learned that real vulnerability requires resourcing. And timing.

That understanding has also deepened how I talk about trauma itself. I know not everyone defines it the same way. Some people still use it to describe the event itself: the car crash, the assault, the loss. But I define it the way my body learned it: not as a moment in time, but as the echo that follows—the way it reshapes how I live, love, trust, and move through the world.

This book isn't a rejection of my earlier work. It's what comes next—the continuation of a conversation I started years ago, but now with steadier hands. It's still rooted in truth, but it's shaped by discernment. There's more pause here. More self-trust. More faith in the timing of what's offered—and what's held close.

See Through is both testimony and tool. I stopped performing what I knew and started trusting it. Where I stopped asking what the world wanted from me and started asking what I was finally ready to give—not from hunger, but from wholeness. I used to believe vulnerability meant sharing everything. Now I understand it differently. Real vulnerability knows what to hold and what to say; not to prove anything, but to live in alignment with yourself. That's what I mean by sovereignty: not control or perfection, but self-trust. The ability to hold your truth without needing to put it on display. To speak—or not speak—from alignment, not obligation. It's the difference between offering something because you choose to, and offering it because you feel you must to belong. Not to be believed. But to be free.

Radical transparency isn't about being sensational or oversharing; it's not exposure for attention. *Performative vulnerability* is transparency without self-trust, truth-telling shaped to be consumed rather than offered from grounded choice. Real vulnerability is truth-telling with self-trust—not to be consumed, but to be whole. Without that trust, sharing too much too soon can drain you, leaving less capacity to care for yourself or anyone else. Vulnerability isn't about being open to the point of collapse; it's about being so rooted in your truth that you no longer feel the need to prove it.

This book doesn't ask for transparency as spectacle or exposure as proof of growth. It asks for grounded, careful attention held by self-trust. *See Through* isn't about being raw to be impressive—it's about being real to be free, offering the kind of truth that doesn't just reveal you, but restores you.

I didn't just restructure how I share. I had to restructure how I heal. Over time, I noticed a pattern—not just in myself, but in the clients, students, and people healing from trauma. Healing doesn't follow a straight line. It moves like a tide: pulling back, pushing forward, reshaping us in layers. And while every story is unique, there's a rhythm that echoes beneath so many of our transformations—one I didn't invent, but one I've lived.

It starts in shame—the quiet, internal kind that teaches you to shrink before you've even found your voice. Then comes the breakthrough: the moment you speak, even if your voice trembles. But telling the truth has a cost. There are relationships that falter, roles that no longer fit, and identities that begin to unravel.

That's where release begins; the painful shedding of what you once clung to for survival. And right behind it, almost always, is grief. Not just for what was lost, but for what was never safe to hold in the first place. Slowly, that grief makes room for integration—the weaving together of past and present, pain and power, without needing to choose one over the other. And finally, you arrive at something deeper than survival. You step into your power—not as an act, but as a homecoming.

That arc—shame, voice, cost, release, grief, integration, power—threads every chapter. Your own arc may bend differently, skip steps, or loop back on itself, but some part of it will likely feel familiar. I won't name the pattern every time, and you might not even notice it at first—but you'll feel it. Because *See Through* isn't structured like a strategy. It's structured like a nervous system, reflecting the emotional terrain we walk when we stop pretending and start returning to ourselves.

To liberate and to love—that's the purpose that anchors me, both in my healing and in how I walk with others in theirs. That purpose has taken many forms over the years: teaching, coaching, writing, learning how to stay when I once would have fled, and learning how to walk away when staying meant self-betrayal. This book is one expression of that purpose. A reclamation. A reminder. A rooted offering to anyone who's ever wondered if telling the truth was worth the cost.

See Through isn't about rawness for attention. It's about realness for liberation. Not to make you impressive; but to help you feel free.

May these pages serve as a mirror, a refuge, and a quiet invitation to return to yourself—unhidden, unarmored, and free. Because liberation is love. And this book is both.

See Through is not a branding exercise. It's a liberation practice—a confrontation with the quiet, exhausting ways we've been taught to perform our pain just to be taken seriously. For too long, visibility has been confused with vulnerability, and vulnerability mistaken for value. But your story is not a transaction. Your truth is not a currency. And your worth is not something that needs to be proven through suffering.

This book won't ask you to bleed to be believed. It won't ask you to collapse to be taken seriously. It invites you to reclaim your voice, your boundaries, and your peace—even in a world that profits from pretending. It's about learning how to be real without sacrificing your emotional safety, and how to live transparently without dissolving into your truth. Because transparency without discernment isn't freedom—it's erosion.

Whether you're reading this in solitude or alongside others who are choosing to live unhidden, the reflections that follow are meant to stir something deeper in you. Not performance, but permission. Not confession, but clarity. You don't have to overshare to be honest. You don't have to empty yourself to be seen. This book is here to honor your pace, and your wholeness.

You'll notice a section called *See Through Reflections* at the end of each chapter. These aren't action steps or journal prompts; they're quiet invitations. Space to pause, turn inward, or spark deeper conversation with people you trust. Whether you're reading this book on your own, in a support group, a classroom, or a leadership circle, these questions are meant to meet you where you are—without performance. Just presence.

This is a personal book. But it's also a deeply collective one. I wrote it for the people who've been labeled "too much" in systems that reward silence. For the ones who ask hard questions in places that have learned to punish dissent. For those who believe that breaking generational cycles means more than healing privately—it means shifting the spaces that keep those cycles intact.

See Through doesn't offer a step-by-step for how to change institutions. But it does offer language—for the quiet ruptures, the self-confrontations, and the brave moments of truth-telling that can ripple outward. If you're reading this with others, I hope it helps you name what's been unspeakable. And if you're reading it alone, I hope it reminds you that you're not.

What this book will offer is a steady lens—one that reflects your truth without demanding your collapse. Whether you're reading this alone or inside a community, I hope these pages give you room to breathe. Permission to stop shrinking. Language for things you've carried without words. And a path back to yourself that doesn't require you to fracture first.

This isn't about confessing everything; it's about reclaiming your voice, your boundaries, and your right to be real—without sacrificing your safety to feel seen.

So welcome. Not just to this book, but to your own truth. This isn't about becoming someone new—it's about remembering who you were before the world taught you to shrink. Before your softness was mistaken for weakness. Before survival became a role you learned to play too well.

May these pages serve as a mirror, a crossroads, and a quiet invitation to return to what was never missing. This isn't a book that demands your rawness. It's a book that reminds you that you have always been whole, even when the world tried to convince you otherwise.

Whether you're reading on your own, in a circle of trusted friends, or within a system still learning how to make space for truth—I hope these words meet you with gentleness. I hope they help you name what's been unspeakable. And most of all, I hope they remind you that you were never too much for the life you want.

Step into *See Through*. What follows isn't a formula; it's a remembering of everything I once silenced to survive, and a return to the voice I almost forgot was mine. May these pages be both window and doorway—a quiet way back to the parts of you that have been waiting to be seen, and a reminder they were never truly lost.

CHAPTER 1

What It Means to Be "See Through"

Before I understood what it meant to be "see through," I spent years performing clarity. I told the truth, often before I was ready to hold it. I spoke openly, even when I didn't feel safe, laying my pain bare before I had the language to understand it. And for a time, I called that honesty. But real transparency—the kind I write about now—isn't just about being visible to others. It's about being willing to truly see yourself.

There were moments—even in healing spaces, the very rooms meant for restoration—where I still swallowed my truth. Not because I didn't have something to say, but because I feared my pain might feel like an inconvenience. I'd scan the group, take the emotional temperature of the room, and ask myself, *Is this too much?* It was reflex. A survival strategy. One I had used so often that silence sometimes felt safer than being seen.

But voice isn't just what you say out loud. It's also what you stop stuffing down. The moment you stop contorting yourself to keep the peace and let your truth rise, even if your voice shakes.

For a long time, I thought the only way to be taken seriously was to make my pain undeniable—to spell it out in sharp detail, to hold nothing back, to turn my truth into proof. That every mention of trauma needed a graphic image, a visible scar, a retelling raw enough to make others understand. But healing showed me something quieter; that truth doesn't have to be a spectacle. I can speak about what I've lived through without staging it. I can name the weight of my experiences without carrying them into every room. I don't owe anyone my rawness to prove my reality.

Radical transparency isn't about saying everything. Being "see through" isn't just letting others look in—it's choosing what to reveal from a place of sovereignty, where self-trust replaces self-erasure. It's speaking what matters without vanishing in the process, and seeing through the patterns you used to survive, the masks you learned to wear, and the voices you swallowed to stay acceptable. This chapter begins there—in the places where I disappeared before I ever knew how to speak.

Before I was ever called brave for telling the truth, I was punished for it. I don't mean physical punishment. I mean the kind that shows up in eye rolls, shushed tones, and door slams. The kind that says, *You're too much,* without using those exact words. *Too sensitive. Too dramatic. Too loud. Too emotional.*

I learned early that big feelings made people uncomfortable. That being expressive meant being a burden. That truth—especially emotional truth—came with consequences.

So I began to scan. Constantly. For tone, for tension, for signs that my presence was too loud or my sadness too heavy. I tried to shrink the volume of who I was, one layer at a time. I learned how to make myself more likable, more helpful, more digestible. I became the child who made the room feel better, even when I didn't feel okay inside it.

I also learned how to over-function. How to hustle for approval through achievement. How to explain myself in twenty different ways just to sound reasonable. How to ignore the quiet voice inside me— the one that said, *You already know*— and defer instead to what others expected. That pattern didn't just show up in my career or relationships. It showed up in how I viewed myself. If I wasn't doing something useful, I didn't believe I had value.

I didn't know it yet, but that was the beginning of my imposter syndrome. Because when you're constantly adjusting who you are to avoid rejection, you lose track of what's real. You start to believe that your worth is conditional. That safety is earned through performance. That love only comes when you're *less* of yourself. And that story doesn't disappear just because you grow up. It shape-shifts.

It shows up in classrooms and boardrooms and friendships—where you smile through discomfort, or apologize before offering an opinion, or spend hours rereading emails because you're afraid you'll sound arrogant or ungrateful. It shows up in therapy, where you name your truth and then immediately try to soften it. It shows up when you do something bold and then spend the next day spiraling—not because you regret it, but because you're afraid you were *too much* again.

That's the root of so many of my survival strategies. The fear that if I show up fully—if I really let myself be seen—something bad will happen. And this fear doesn't only shape personal relationships; it shapes teams, classrooms, and cultures. I've watched entire organizations operate like this: people holding their breath, staying silent, nodding through discomfort because the cost of honesty feels too high.

So, when people now say I'm brave for being transparent, what they don't always realize is this: I'm still punished for it. Just like I was back then. The eye rolls. The distance. The discomfort people don't name but make me feel anyway. I haven't outgrown the consequences; I've just stopped shrinking to avoid them.

The bravery isn't in telling the truth once. It's in choosing not to disappear afterward, even when others wish I would.

Being "see through" isn't about being raw for applause. It's about taking back the parts of yourself that once had to disappear to be safe. And that work always begins with shame—not the shame others placed on you, but the shame you internalized just to stay acceptable.

I've always been the one to say what others were afraid to. Not because I thought I was right. Not because I wanted attention. But because I could feel the tension in the room—the silent frustration, the swallowed truth—and my body couldn't hold it in. If no one else was going to say it, I would. Staff meetings were one of the places this happened most.

I could feel the discomfort sitting in people's shoulders. I could hear the unsaid questions hanging in the silence after every vague directive. I watched the way colleagues glanced at each other when something didn't make sense—or worse, when something felt harmful—and how they'd look down again just as quickly. The air always got thick in those moments. And I'd break it.

I'd raise my hand. Ask the hard question. Offer the perspective no one wanted to say out loud, even though I knew I wasn't the only one thinking it. Sometimes, someone would join me—usually quietly, and only after I broke the silence first. More often, I'd get the nods, the hallway thank-yous, the private messages. And just as often, I'd get the backlash—the eye rolls, the passive-aggressive emails, the sudden distance from people who once acted like friends.

That's the thing about being honest in public: the people who agree with you don't always stand beside you. They stand behind you—quietly—while you absorb the risk. Whether it's a team meeting, a family dinner, or a community forum, the one who speaks the uncomfortable truth often becomes the lightning rod. Others may nod in private, but few will shoulder the discomfort in the open. And in that gap, silence keeps winning.

I never spoke up to be a hero. I spoke because silence made my skin crawl—because pretending not to notice harm felt like betrayal, not just of myself, but of everyone else swallowing their truth to stay safe. I know what it's like to sit in that silence, hoping someone will speak on your behalf, and realizing no one will. If someone had done that for me when I was young, maybe some of the harm would have been spared. I can't rewrite that part of my story. But I can make sure I'm not another quiet bystander in someone else's.

Being see through in those moments isn't about exposure. It's about integrity—refusing to collude with the lie that everything is fine when it isn't. It's about trusting that clarity, even if it's unwelcome, is still kinder than complicity.

I didn't always do it gracefully. I'm sure I was labeled reactive, emotional, even unprofessional. And maybe sometimes I was. But I've since learned: telling the truth doesn't always look polished. It looks like trembling hands. A dry mouth. A shaking voice. But it's still truth. And it still matters.

But before I ever told the truth out loud, I learned how to hide it.

I didn't just grow up trying to be a high achiever. I grew up trying to be good—the kind of girl who never made anyone uncomfortable. The kind who smiled more than she spoke, who softened her opinions to keep the peace. I learned to read the room and shape-shift to match it.

If the moment called for a showman, I performed—telling stories, laughing loudly, dancing like I wasn't carrying anything heavy. If someone needed stillness, I offered that too—sitting quietly with them at a table while the rest of the party moved around us like we were in a different universe. I could blend into a crowd or command it, depending on what felt safest, or most useful.

I didn't plan these shifts. They happened automatically. I'd watch how others moved, how they joked or stayed silent, how they carried themselves—and I'd adjust without thinking. My sister Christina used to call me a chameleon. Once, we were shopping with our other sister Nicole when I ran into one of my students. Afterward, Christina pointed out how my voice and body language had shifted—how I slipped into slang and mannerisms that mirrored the student's energy without even realizing I'd done it. At the time, I took it as a sign of connection. What I didn't yet see was how often connection came at the cost of knowing who I actually was.

I thought it meant I was adaptable. Safe. Skilled at connection. But what I didn't realize was that this wasn't connection—it was a role I kept playing.

Being good wasn't just a family script. It was a cultural survival strategy. It meant swallowing my discomfort so no one else had to feel theirs. It meant managing the emotions in the room like a second job. It meant looking strong, even when I was falling apart. And the longer I performed that version of me, the more I lost touch with myself.

That strategy doesn't just play out in families. It gets reinforced in systems—in schools that reward compliance over courage, in workplaces that label emotion as unprofessional, in leadership models that prize likability more than truth. We don't just learn to adapt ourselves for individuals; we learn to appease institutions. And sometimes, even after years of unlearning those patterns, one unexpected moment can bring them roaring back.

If it seems like Vietnam comes up a lot in this book, that's because I wrote most of it there—while traveling, healing, and reflecting in the wake of a major life transition. Nearly every chapter was shaped in some way by the things I experienced or unpacked during that time. Including this one.

I was on a tour to Cần Giờ Monkey Island—real monkeys, jumping onto backpacks, stealing glasses. It was chaotic and almost comical—until one sprinted toward me. I flinched, unsure if it would bite, jump, or pass by. I didn't scream. I didn't panic. I just braced.

The second time, I caught a glimpse of it from behind, just before it touched my leg with both hands. At least the first one had been in plain sight. This one came out of nowhere, and the jolt of it hit something deep in my nervous system. I flinched and screamed—a sharp, instinctive sound I couldn't suppress, my whole body snapping tight before I even registered what had happened.

That's when an older American man in my group turned to me and said, "I didn't expect you to be a victim." He wasn't joking. As a former pastor and prison volunteer, he explained people are victimized because they carry themselves like victims—it's about what they project.

It hit a raw nerve. Even now, part of me still fears he might be right. Part of me still wonders if there's something in me that invites harm—a flaw, a weakness, a sign stamped on my back. The same fear I've carried since childhood, when I was told repeatedly—through words and wounds—that something was wrong with me. Too much. Or not enough.

I looked down and quietly said, "I've actually been assaulted multiple times." What I didn't say—but felt in every part of my body— was the shame. The shame of speaking up and still feeling unseen. The shame of having to justify a scream. The shame of that old, lingering belief: Maybe there is something wrong with me.

Yet there I was—a full-grown woman with a PhD—shrinking under the weight of one stranger's opinion. Someone who didn't know my story, or that I'd survived everything from sexual violence to being attacked from behind at knifepoint. Someone who had no idea how many years I spent wondering if I was to blame. That's what shame does. It doesn't care how far you've come; it only needs one moment to pull you back.

Moments like this aren't unique to travel—they follow you into offices, classrooms, even your own home. Different settings, same crossroads: someone assumes authority over your truth, and you must decide whether to shrink or speak. That's exactly why reclaiming voice matters, because shame thrives in the spaces where you've been silenced. It waits for the smallest opening to take the mic back.

When it happened on Monkey Island, I could have left it there—another moment filed under *proof I'm still too much*. But instead, I reached for something I didn't have in earlier seasons: perspective I could trust. And with it came words I hadn't always been able to find—not defensive or apologetic, but steady and clear—the kind that make space for truth without handing it over for judgment.

What helped me reclaim that moment was a conversation later with my friend David, who's known me for years. He reminded me of what had really changed in my life: not just my mindset, but my environment. I left the toxic town I grew up in. I stopped drinking. I stopped surrounding myself with chaos. And the violence stopped, too. I wasn't a magnet for pain. I was just stuck in places where pain was normalized.

And the kicker? The same man who called me a victim had his glasses stolen twice by the monkeys—despite multiple warnings. The second time, he turned to me angrily, mid-chaos, and asked why I hadn't warned him. As if it were my job to protect him. As if his humiliation needed an outlet, and I was the easiest one to blame.

So let me get this straight: If I get touched or attacked, it's because I'm "playing the victim." But if he gets attacked, it's my fault for not preventing it?

He didn't just lose his glasses twice—the guide had to barter food to get them back—he also went home with mud and monkey prints on his fanny pack, shirt, and face. Meanwhile, I didn't lose a single item. And somehow, I was still the one he labeled a victim.

Even now, I feel a flash of anger—not just at him, but at myself. For how quickly I let his words shrink me. For how easily I slipped back into the old reflex of shame. People like this man have been trying to make me feel small for as long as I can remember. And still, my first instinct was to question myself.

That's why reflecting on moments like these—and having friends like David who help me reframe them—matters. It's how I see my story more clearly. It's how I take my power back.

Because I've since realized that shame doesn't only come from trauma. It comes from pretending. From all the tiny, daily ways you contort your truth to fit what's expected. From constantly recalibrating your tone, your emotion, your presence—until you no longer know which version of you is real.

That performance starts young. And it doesn't always look dramatic—sometimes it looks like showing up to class with a blank stare, pretending not to care, because caring too much would expose how lost you feel inside. Sometimes it looks like giving up before you've even tried, because hope feels too dangerous to hold.

By the end of ninth grade, I wasn't expecting much for my future. My grades were low; my self-worth even lower. I didn't see the point in trying—not in school, not in life. I had been through more than most adults could fathom, and I was tired of pretending I was fine. Given the abuse and degradation I'd endured, I didn't think I was smart. I'd been told too many times that I was stupid, that I'd never amount to anything.

Even years later, after earning advanced degrees and teaching complex science courses at the college level, I still struggled to believe otherwise. I can't count how many times in adulthood someone has looked at me in surprise and said, "I don't know how you don't know that." Most of the time, they didn't mean it casually. For survival, I'd spent a lifetime studying people—reading the flicker in their eyes, the shift in their tone, the subtle tightening in their shoulders. I knew when a comment carried judgment.

Because I come across as accomplished and put together, people expect flawlessness. How dare I call myself a professor, an author, a world traveler if, in their eyes, I haven't earned that right? Each remark pressed on the same old bruise—the belief that I wasn't enough, that I was still the girl who didn't measure up. These moments aren't random. They show up in different arenas, wearing different faces, but the pattern is always the same: a collision between my voice and the systems or people invested in keeping it small.

Early on, all I knew was how to work hard. How to survive. How to follow rules and stay out of the way. I didn't believe I had a voice that mattered—or a future that could hold something good.

That began to change the summer between ninth and tenth grade, when I joined Upward Bound, a college prep program for low-income, first-generation students. For six weeks I lived in a college dorm, took classes that prepared us not just for higher education but for the belief that we belonged there. I met students from towns I'd never seen, spent a week in Maine, went white-water rafting for the first time, and inched across a ropes course that made my whole body shake.

My world, once confined to a small town where most families had never left, suddenly widened in every direction. I saw more ways to live, more ways to think, more possibilities than I'd ever imagined. And I wanted more. That hunger gave me not only hope, but a sense of direction—a pull toward the wider world that would later shape everything, including my determination to travel and experience as much diversity in people, places, and ideas as I could.

When I returned to school that fall, I studied harder, raised my hand in class, and imagined what it might feel like to be proud of myself. I kept going back to Upward Bound every summer for three years, and it anchored me. It showed me what I was capable of.

By the end of tenth grade, I had pulled my grades up enough to be inducted into the National Honor Society. Eventually, I earned the title of Salutatorian—second in my class. It should have been a triumphant moment. But when the school administrator delivered the news, he immediately added, "Don't get too excited. The boy who thought he would get the title is going to be upset."

He said it the moment he saw a smile start to form—as if my joy needed to be managed, softened, trimmed back down to size. No "congratulations." No "you earned this." Just another warning to shrink.

That moment stays with me—not because it was surprising, but because it confirmed a pattern I already knew too well: the minute I started to rise, someone tried to put me back in my place. But by then, I had learned something that couldn't be unlearned—that education was my key to choice, that stepping into my voice was no longer optional, and that pride in myself wasn't something to apologize for. It was something I had clawed my way toward, piece by painful piece.

I still find it astonishing when I look at my life as a whole—not through the lens of a single story, but as a collection. What stands out isn't just the number of hardships, but their range. This isn't one storyline with a single villain playing different roles. It's a patchwork quilt of challenges stitched across decades: personal, professional, physical, cultural, relational.

When I see them together, I understand why people sometimes tilt their heads in disbelief. How can so much happen to one person? They don't mean the joy—they mean grief, the violations, the betrayals.

For years, I thought it meant something was wrong with me, that I carried a flaw or mark that drew harm like a magnet. But now I see it differently. I've lived in more environments, cultures, and situations than most people will ever touch. That kind of exposure doesn't just raise the odds of wonder—it raises the odds of wounds. I've also spoken up when others stayed silent, and set boundaries where others let the line slide. In spaces built on silence, that choice often comes with backlash. And I've taken chances most people sidestep, walking into arenas where the stakes—and risks—are higher.

Most people's adversity repeats familiar patterns. Mine has spanned continents, systems, hierarchies, intimate relationships, professional power plays, and my own body. And I don't look away. Many people numb, normalize, or forget. I notice. I feel the weight. I remember. That makes the load heavier, but also the meaning richer.

I don't share this to compare lives or rank pain. This isn't about competition; it's about context. If you find yourself wondering later how one woman could hold this much in her history, know that I've wondered too. What I've come to believe is this: living differently attracts more of everything—the resistance, the connection, the transformation, the truth. And while the cost can be steep, the return is even greater. The same life that's brought me face-to-face with so much loss has also brought me face-to-face with myself. And that's a meeting I wouldn't trade.

I've also learned that living differently means returning, again and again, to the same crossroads: disappear or speak. You'll see that choice threaded through every chapter of this book, each time wearing a different face. And while the cost of speaking can be high, it's nothing compared to the cost of silence.

Still, living this way doesn't mean the barriers fall away. Even now—in this exact moment of writing *See Through*— I find myself running into walls when I try to tell the truth.

Recently, I decided to share one of my most traumatic experiences for integration into Chapter 6 with ChatGPT. It took everything in me to put those words down. But the first time I sent it, the system flagged it as a "policy violation." I edited. Tried again. Flagged again. Over and over. The safety filter was doing its job—but in that moment, it felt like another door closing on what I could say, a smaller version of the gatekeeping this chapter is naming.

With each red warning, the tightness in my chest increased, my heart sinking further. It was like being told repeatedly: This is too much. You're too much. When I finally did get a response, the message itself was still blocked from view. The irony wasn't lost on me—a book about radical transparency being met with invisible gates.

It gave me an unexpected clarity about why these experiences have cut so deep. If even a computer system can't hold them, how on earth was I supposed to? How was I ever expected to carry all these stories without breaking?

Oddly, that thought brought a strange lightness. It made all the destructive ways I once tried to cope feel less like weakness, and more like inevitability. Of course I needed somewhere for all of it to go. And if a machine can't hold my truth, maybe there's nothing "wrong" with me for struggling to.

And it's not just ChatGPT. I've had Facebook flag posts for "violating standards" when I spoke plainly about trauma. Different platforms, same message: truth invited, then penalized. The methods change—an algorithm, a policy, a community's unspoken rules—but the effect is the same: truth gets gated. Every time, it's a reminder of how hard it is to name the things that have shaped me.

And yet, here I am—still naming them. Still pressing "send." Not because it's easy, but because each time we speak through the barriers, their grip weakens. Every truth voiced plants a marker in the silence, so the next person who tries won't have to feel quite so alone.

That's been true in more than just writing this book. The moments when I've pushed through resistance—when I've chosen to step forward instead of shrink—have often led to the greatest turning points in my life. Some of the earliest returns came from opportunities I never could have imagined when I was younger; the kind that cracked the door open to a different future. One of the most pivotal was Upward Bound. It didn't just prepare me for college; it helped me rewrite the script of who I was allowed to be. The trembling on a ropes course, the rush of white-water, the awe of a dorm room that looked nothing like home—those embodied memories became proof my mind couldn't ignore. Belonging wasn't just an idea anymore. It had texture, memory, weight. I went on to earn three degrees, taught college courses, and worked in higher education policy. But more than the titles or accomplishments, what mattered most was this: I started to trust my potential, even when others couldn't see it.

That shift wasn't loud or dramatic at first. It began quietly, with a refusal to keep living like I was invisible. Being "see through" didn't start with telling my whole story out loud. It started with something smaller but just as radical: not letting shame have the final word.

This chapter is about finding your voice beneath the roles you learned to play—about facing the shame that comes not just from what was done to you, but from what you taught yourself to do to survive. Not louder, but truer. The voice that doesn't ask permission to exist.

For a long time, that act kept me safe. Eventually, it took other forms, more dangerous ones. But it started here: with the belief that being acceptable mattered more than being real.

And what we accept in ourselves, we often replicate in our communities. When we pretend instead of telling the truth, we unintentionally reinforce the silence—teaching others that safety depends on invisibility. But every unspoken truth costs more than we realize. And every honest voice, even the trembling ones, makes collective honesty more possible.

I've been acting since I was a child, not on a stage but in every room that asked me to make myself smaller. One of the most practiced acts I ever mastered was the smile. Not the joyful kind, but the one that smooths over tension, erases discomfort, and makes other people feel safe even when I don't. It's the smile that says, "I'm fine," before I've even had time to ask myself if that's true.

For a long time, I believed I smiled because I was friendly. The truth is, I smiled because I thought it was safer than being honest. It became automatic. I smiled when I was hurt. I smiled when I was overwhelmed. I smiled when I wanted to scream. For years, no one knew the difference, because I didn't let them. I was too well-practiced. Smiling made me seem strong, approachable, pleasant—but it also made me invisible.

There was a time when I walked into my office every morning and greeted everyone with a cheerful "Good morning!" even on days when I felt like my soul was shattering. Then one day, I came in silently. I sat at my desk, trying to focus, barely holding it together. A colleague walked by a little while later and said, "Oh, I didn't know you were here. I didn't hear you say, 'Good morning.' I look forward to that each morning."

I know she meant it kindly. But what she didn't realize was that she was reinforcing the very thing that was eroding me: the expectation that I show up smiling, no matter how much I'm hurting.

What she didn't know is that at 13, when I finally spoke up about being sexually abused, someone I trusted told me that if I couldn't grow up and control my emotions, I wasn't welcome back to their home. From that point on, I learned to stuff my sadness into the darkest corners of myself and shine bright enough to make everyone else comfortable.

After that day at work, I started smiling again at the office door—not because I felt okay, but because I was still trying to protect others from my pain. That's the thing about emotional performance; sometimes the parts you use to protect yourself become the very things that erase you.

I feel the same way about being called a *survivor*. I know many people embrace that word—even draw strength from it—and I would never take that from them. But for me, it's shorthand that turns a complex, ongoing reality into a palatable story—one they can nod at and move on from. It reminds me of all the times my experience was reduced to something easier for others to digest, all the times I was expected to fit into a version of myself that felt safer for them.

That doesn't mean I reject the truth: I *am* a survivor, and it took everything I had to live through what I've lived through. I'm proud of that. I just refuse to let the word define me. Naming me after the worst things that have happened to me keeps me tethered to the past. I'd rather be known for what I've *become*: an author, a professor, an adventurer, an entrepreneur.

That's the truth I want to carry forward. And part of carrying it forward means accepting that not every moment of visibility will be on my terms. I can own my story, but I can't script every scene; being see through means choosing the truths I share and accepting the ones I didn't choose. Sometimes life reveals you in ways you never intended. And sometimes those reveals aren't profound or brave at all—they're simply ridiculous.

Like the morning I left Japan for Thailand when I was running late and sprinting with my luggage. Somewhere between "I can still make it" and "Oh no, I can't," I tripped. Not just a little stumble—a full wipeout in the middle of a busy walkway. And because the universe has a sense of humor, I was wearing a dress. It flew up, and an entire crowd of strangers got a full view of my, thankfully, very modest underwear.

I scrambled to my feet, muttering a mix of apologies and nervous laughter, silently praying no one had been recording. I could just imagine ending up on one of those silly travel blooper reels—a backpacker in sensible shoes and not-so-sensible haste.

Moments like that are humbling. They strip away the illusion that you can ever fully control how you're seen. You can prepare, plan, and position yourself—and still end up flashing an unsuspecting group of commuters on a Sunday morning in Tokyo.

And maybe that's part of what "being see through" really means. Not just telling your truth on purpose, but staying human when life accidentally puts you on display.

The funny stories are easier to share. They roll off your tongue without much risk. But there's another kind of exposure—the quiet, unchosen kind—that can feel far more vulnerable.

It wasn't just my smile that masked the pain. I masked it with motion too—with noise, productivity, and overgiving. For a long time, stillness felt like a threat. It took me years to even realize I was doing it. To notice how often I defaulted to cheerfulness when I was actually drowning. How I'd soften my tone, nod along, and hold back the truth just to avoid making someone uncomfortable. I thought that made me kind. But it wasn't kindness. It was self-erasure.

Even when my traumas were at their worst, I smiled. I was bubbly. Cheerful. Upbeat. On the outside, I looked like a kid with nothing to hide. That smile helped me survive. It helped me hold onto the hope that maybe—just maybe—the whole world wasn't dangerous. But it also confused people. It still does. Some don't believe my story because I don't look broken enough to them. As if trauma only counts when it leaves visible scars. They don't see how much that smile cost me. How it became both a shield and a silencer. How I learned to wear happiness to make other people more comfortable with my pain.

I've since learned that real safety doesn't come from being pleasant. It comes from being present. And sometimes, presence means not smiling. It means letting the tension stay in the room. Letting the truth rise. Letting myself be fully seen, not just accepted.

For a long time, I feared silence more than chaos. Stillness made space for thoughts I didn't want to face. So I filled every moment—with food, with movement, with noise. If I wasn't working, I was walking. If I wasn't walking, I was cleaning. If I wasn't cleaning, I was scrolling or snacking or planning my next big thing. I didn't know how to sit still—not because I didn't have time, but because I was afraid of what might surface when I did.

It wasn't until I began practicing yoga and meditation that I learned stillness could be safe. That I could let difficult thoughts rise without being swallowed by them. That silence didn't have to mean loneliness; it could mean clarity.

Yoga didn't just teach me how to stretch or breathe. It taught me how to *listen*. To my body. To my emotions. To the stories I had been running from for years. It gave me the courage to stop distracting myself long enough to *feel*— without needing to fix it, numb it, or explain it away.

That's what voice is too. It's not always the thing you say out loud. Sometimes, it's the thing you stop running from. The truth you stop avoiding. The version of yourself you're finally willing to face—even when it hurts. One truth I could finally face in that stillness was this: I had used sex not to connect, but to disappear. I wasn't chasing pleasure. I was chasing erasure.

Promiscuity wasn't a phase. It wasn't rebellion. It was grief. It was trauma. It was self-destruction dressed up as connection.

It started when I was a teenager—during the worst years of the sexual abuse—and it escalated after my partner Stan died. I was 25 and completely shattered. After finding him dead, I moved into the house we were supposed to be moving into together—a place that felt like a monument to everything we'd lost. At the same time, I had started talking about the sexual trauma I experienced as a child and teenager for the first time in my life. It was too much to hold. My body was alive, but everything inside me felt like it was unraveling.

I wasn't trying to feel better. I was trying to feel different—even if it was just a different kind of pain. I had unprotected sex with random men I met in bars. I didn't love them. I didn't even like most of them.

But for a few hours, they gave me something to focus on that wasn't grief or emptiness or the crushing sense that I didn't deserve to be alive.

One night at a local bar, I was playing pool—something I'd gotten good at after becoming a regular. I loved the game, but I loved even more how it gave me a chance to show off my big personality and make men notice me. That night, a man I'd just met grinned and said, "Let's make a bet. If I win, I get to come home with you." I smiled and said yes. I liked that he even wanted me to make that bet. By then, I'd put on quite a bit of weight, and my self-esteem had plummeted. Any scrap of proof that I was still desirable felt like oxygen. But when he won, I realized I didn't actually want him in my bed. I thought it was stupid that I'd traded my body in a game of pool—and I felt that same way when I invited him into my home, while we were having sex, after he left, and even now.

Looking back, I see it differently. It wasn't just a bad decision. I was using my body as currency, trying to buy a sense that my existence mattered, if only for a moment. To stop myself from crying while he was inside me, I told myself over and over: at least he wants to touch me. At least I'm not too disgusting to be touched. It still breaks my heart that that's what I held onto—that my heart was breaking in real time, and the only way I knew to survive was to cling to the smallest sign I wasn't worthless.

I couldn't bring myself to end my life, but I secretly hoped someone else would. That one of the men I picked up might hurt me, kill me, or give me something that would. I didn't care about protection. I didn't care about myself. I just wanted to escape the person I was when I was alone.

There wasn't silence in my head. There were screams. Flashbacks. Echoes. I was grieving one of the only people who ever made me feel safe while reliving years of being violated by people who didn't. My mind felt like a war zone, and sex was the only thing I could reach for that briefly cut through the chaos.

For a long time, I didn't try to stop. I was barely surviving. I couldn't work, and I rarely left the house. When I did, it was usually to find someone who would sleep with me so I didn't have to feel so alone. At home, I binged constantly—eating enormous amounts of food without trying to undo the damage like I used to. My eating disorder had begun years earlier, when I was 12 and the abuse escalated. Back then, food was the first thing I could control. If I couldn't change how exposed I felt, I could at least change how small I was. Smaller meant safer. Smaller meant praised. I wasn't hungry for food—I was hungry for approval.

After Stan died, everything shifted. I wasn't trying to control the pain anymore. I was letting it consume me. The disorder stopped being about shrinking; it became about numbing.

I carried an unbearable amount of shame. Shame for how I used sex to punish myself, and food to numb myself. Shame for knowing what I was doing and doing it anyway. Shame for not being able to stop. I hated how much I needed comfort, how much I needed to feel wanted, even if it came through destruction. I believed the size of my body said something about the size of my failure. That I was broken. Disgusting. Unworthy of love. But none of that was true. I wasn't seeking pleasure. I was seeking proof that I still mattered in a world where I felt invisible.

Eventually, something in me shifted. Not overnight. Not because I suddenly loved myself. But because I was exhausted. I was tired of feeling empty. Tired of chasing validation that never lasted. Tired of pretending that any of this made me feel whole.

The first shift I made was letting go of the men who made me feel worse. If the connection was going to be casual, it at least had to be kind. That wasn't self-love, but it was a boundary—and at the time, that was something. Around the same time, I started hiking. Not because I wanted to, and not out of some sudden burst of self-care. The bingeing had pushed my weight to 222 pounds, and the physical consequences were getting harder to ignore—high cholesterol, sleep apnea, and the quiet fear that my body was beginning to shut down. I wasn't ready to give up food as comfort, and I couldn't force myself to exercise just because it was good for me. I've never liked movement for the sake of movement—it had to feel natural. And walking always had. I used to walk a lot when I was younger. I grew up in the Adirondack Park in New York, so returning to hiking felt like reclaiming something I used to know—a quiet, familiar way of coping that didn't hurt. It wasn't about joy at first. It was about survival. It was the only thing that gave me even a flicker of peace.

But over time, my reasons changed. Every time I finished a hike— no matter how small—I felt a sliver of pride. And eventually, I started chasing that feeling instead. My body got stronger. I got stronger. Slowly, I stopped needing strangers to make me feel seen—because I was starting to see myself. And the more I saw myself, the more I could speak for the girl I'd been—not in apology, but in ownership.

But even the rituals that give us our voice can change—sometimes without our consent. In the summer of 2024, I found out just how severe the degeneration in my spine really was. I'd always known my body had limits. But I hadn't expected this: the end of mountain summits—the kind that once saved me.

Those climbs weren't just hobbies. They were lifelines. Mountains were the first places I learned to breathe again after trauma. They taught me how to stay with myself—how to push through fear without abandoning my truth. They were where I felt most alive, most free, most like myself.

Losing that wasn't just a physical grief. It was spiritual. If I couldn't return to the peaks that once steadied me, I had to find new landscapes that could. And if I couldn't speak in the language of summits anymore, I would have to find new ways to give my voice shape—to claim it in places where strength looked different but mattered just as much.

That realization is part of what pushed me to finally pursue my dream of full-time travel in 2025—a different kind of adventure. One that honored my body instead of demanding its sacrifice. One that still let me feel wild, but in a way I could sustain.

That's how I ended up in Thailand. Volunteering at an elephant sanctuary had been on my list for over a decade. I thought it would be a beautiful way to begin this next chapter—a quieter but still meaningful kind of strength. But I didn't yet know—as I'll share in the next chapter—how much it would ask of me. Or how much I was still willing to give, even when it hurt. I had been here before—in different seasons, under different griefs—quietly recognizing that certain versions of me were already gone.

There was a walk I took one afternoon through the cemetery near my old home. I remember thinking about the habits and beliefs I wouldn't want to die with, and realizing promiscuity hadn't been part of my life for a long time. That version of me had already passed. And I wasn't mourning her. I could finally honor her because I understood why she existed. She wasn't weak. She wasn't shameful. She was doing everything she could to survive. And I'm still here because she did.

For years, I thought the worst thing people could do was judge me for the ways I'd coped. Now I know the real danger is letting that fear decide what parts of me get to be seen. I spent decades shrinking to fit, offering only the versions of myself that were easy to digest. That shame was a weight I carried for so long I believed it might break me. But speaking the hard parts out loud—even knowing they may be misunderstood—is how I reclaim my voice. I won't share every detail of my past in this book, but the pieces I do share, especially the most uncomfortable ones, are here because I refuse to keep silencing myself for the comfort of people who've never lived a fraction of what I've endured. I have one precious life, and tragedy has already shaped too much of it. I won't give another ounce of it to anyone who means me harm.

Some will judge me for the stories I tell. But it's easy to judge the version of me who slept with men to feel whole if you've never lived inside her body. She wasn't broken. She was adapting to a world that made her feel disposable—surviving the only way she knew how. Once I stopped shaming her, I could finally see her clearly. And the more clearly I saw her, the more I could speak for her—not in apology, but in ownership.

I used to look at birds with envy—not just for their wings, but for what they represented: freedom, escape, the ability to rise above it all. During some of the hardest seasons of my life, I'd stretch my arms out like wings when the wind blew against me, as if I could will myself into flight. The longing wasn't for adventure—it was for release. I didn't want to soar for the thrill of it. I wanted to fly because I didn't know how to stay.

But now, after everything, I'm learning that freedom doesn't always come from leaving. Sometimes it comes from choosing not to disappear. From staying with myself—fully, finally—and seeing through every version I once had to become.

That's what this book is about. Not just telling the truth—but learning what it really costs. And deciding to do it anyway.

See Through Reflections

1. Personal Reflection

- When was the first time you chose silence over truth to avoid consequences—and what did that silence cost you?

- Have you ever been judged for not knowing something others assumed you "should" know? How did that moment affect your sense of worth?

- What did you learn as a child about the risks of being "too much"—in voice, ambition, or emotion? How does that training still influence you now?

2. Group or Cultural Exploration

- How do you perform "being okay" in spaces that reward composure or compliance—your workplace, your family, your community?

- Whose truth gets heard in your environment? Whose emotions get labeled as excessive, unstable, or inconvenient?

- How does your organization, classroom, or circle respond to people who speak up about harm? What would need to shift for telling the truth to feel safer than silence?

3. Somatic/Embodied Practice

- Recall a recent moment you smiled, minimized, or softened your truth to make others more comfortable. Where did it land in your body? What might it feel like to release that mask— even for a single breath?

- Place a hand over your heart or your gut—wherever truth lives for you—and say aloud: "I'm allowed to be real, even when it challenges expectations." Notice what rises. Let yourself sit with it, without rushing to soothe or explain it away.

CHAPTER 2

The Double-Edged Sword of Being Real

In August 2025, while finishing the final chapters of this book, I volunteered at a Buddhist monastery in Taiwan. I didn't go just to serve—I went to see if immersing myself in a spiritual community, especially one rooted in mindfulness and nonjudgment, might offer the sense of belonging I'd craved for most of my life.

I've always been open to religion. I see its value—the ritual, the rhythm, the communal care. And for most of my life, I've longed to be part of something bigger than myself. Not just individual friendships, but a collective. A home. Growing up, I couldn't relate to kids my age. I had to mature too quickly, forced into roles I wasn't ready for. By my teens, I was surviving what no one should have to. In my twenties, I was still grasping for something steady—reliving past traumas while grieving the loss of my partner. I clung to people, institutions, belief systems. Anything that helped me stay anchored. And even as I stabilized in my thirties, let healthier people in, built a life I was proud of—the ache to belong never really left.

Religion seemed like the most obvious place to look. It offered a ready-made community. Shared values. And depending on the group, a focus on compassion and care. But every time I joined a religious space, something about me always seemed to disqualify me from fully belonging. I either knew I'd need to hide parts of myself, or I was told outright that those parts weren't welcome.

In my thirties, I thought I'd finally found the right fit. A community of Christian sisters invited me to become a lay associate, and I loved being among women who were grounded, spunky, and devoted to justice. But a man—another lay associate—who led many of the activities I was involved in started pulling me back into that old performance trap. He kept trying to mold me into a version of myself that aligned with his interpretation of the community's values. He wasn't clergy. He wasn't a nun. But he became a mouthpiece for the parts of the group that valued conformity over authenticity. And eventually, just like so many times before, I started shrinking.

His presence, and his need to reel me in, took the joy out of the experience. And that mattered, because joy has been hard-won in my life. Survival has marked most of my years, not lightness. Here he was, dimming something sacred. He didn't just take my confidence; he also took a community I'd fought to find. To stay involved as I had would've meant more than adapting; it would've meant disappearing. So instead, I pulled back. I didn't leave entirely, but I chose to shrink my role in the community rather than shrink myself. Still, the loss stung. It felt like a familiar loss at the hands of a man with influence. And the cost wasn't abstract: fewer service opportunities, fewer gatherings, fewer touchpoints of belonging. Choosing my voice meant surrendering a community I'd fought to find.

After that, I turned to other forms of belonging—hiking groups, volunteer work, spiritual retreats. I kept searching for that perfect mix of structure and safety. I wanted something that would let me show up fully, without needing to perform. Buddhism had fascinated me since I was a teenager, and I admired its emphasis on presence, compassion, and non-attachment. So when I applied to the monastery program in Taiwan, I did it with cautious hope. I knew it wouldn't be easy, but I believed it would be kind.

It wasn't unkind; it was different than I imagined, and my history made that difference feel sharp.

The monastery grounds were peaceful, and the people sincere. Many international volunteers raved about their experience, and I could see why. But for me, the environment felt more triggering than tranquil. It wasn't physically unsafe, but it pressed on every bruise I thought had already healed.

Volunteers were expected not just to help, but to live in alignment with the monastic rhythm and the Five Precepts: no killing, stealing, sexual misconduct, false speech, or intoxicants. In their simplest form, that also meant such things as respecting resources—not wasting food, electricity, or other people's time. Layered on top of that were monastery rules: no speaking during meals, no deviation from the schedule. A discipline master with a microphone would walk through the dining hall in case reminders were needed about silence or phone use. I never heard him correct anyone, but the mere presence of someone watching, waiting, ready to intervene activated something deep in me. I became hypervigilant. My perfectionism flared. I monitored every move I made, every glance, every sound. Not because I wanted praise, but because I was terrified of doing something wrong. Of being told I didn't belong. Again.

And eventually, that's exactly what happened.

On the fourth day, I decided I would leave after lunch the following day. I'd planned to stay two full weeks, but my body had already told me it wasn't sustainable. Still, I showed up fully for my duties that day. I moved slowly and deliberately, taking extra care in the heat to do everything right. I wanted to contribute, to leave gracefully, to prove—if only to myself—that I could follow through with integrity.

At one point, the nun overseeing our cleaning duties, clearly frustrated that I was new and needed guidance, handed me her phone with a translated message: "It looks like you don't do this kind of work very often."

Maybe it was a simple observation, but it broke something in me. I was already exhausted, already fighting back the old voices. And now I had confirmation that even my best effort hadn't been enough—not in outcome, but in impression. It didn't matter that I'd stayed late. That I'd taken my duties seriously and followed every rule. I still didn't measure up. The cost that week was real: sleepless nights, hypervigilance, and leaving early to protect a nervous system already frayed.

In that moment, I wasn't just reacting to a comment. I was reliving a lifetime of not-enoughness. My brain knew it wasn't abuse. But my body didn't. My body heard: *You're failing. You're bad. You don't belong.* My body buzzed with shame. Braced for rejection. Shrunk.

Others might have chalked it up to cultural differences—and yes, some of it was. One of my fellow volunteers said she was trying to see it that way too, choosing to overlook certain moments so she could focus on the bigger benefits of the experience. But in my body, trauma doesn't care about cultural nuance. It registers tone, power dynamics, microjudgments—familiar patterns. It remembers.

I started to spiral. Were the passing comments about how people tend to lose weight during the program meant for me? Were they watching my body? Judging what I ate? It replicated so many dynamics from my past—the subtle shaming, the measuring of my worth through performance, even the quiet undercurrent of not being slim or pretty enough for certain men. I talk more about my relationships with men later in this book, but the roots of that same judgment were here, too, just dressed in different clothes. I thought of the two airline staff at an airport in China two months before who pointed at my stomach and laughed. Sometimes people speak in code. Sometimes they don't need to. My mind raced: Should I explain that

I'm in eating disorder recovery? That I'm not "indulging"—I'm surviving?

The old perfectionism kept pressing: *Why couldn't I make this work? Why couldn't I be like the other volunteers?*

And then I remembered: I built this life so I wouldn't have to shape-shift. I left conventional work so I wouldn't have to bury myself just to meet someone else's demands. Yet here I was, unpaid, trying to earn approval from people I didn't even know.

The monastery didn't break me. It mirrored me. It showed me how easily I still fall into old patterns—seeking validation, striving for perfection, internalizing blame. It reminded me why I've always been sensitive to rigid systems. Because for me, structure has rarely been neutral. It has been a place of pressure. Of punishment. Of feeling small.

In the end, I still left a donation. Not out of guilt, but gratitude— because even though the experience wasn't what I'd hoped for, it gave me exactly what I needed: clarity. I saw where I still contort myself for approval. I saw how far I've come, and where I still have work to do. Most of all, I saw that even a space that seems holy can still wound you if it demands you disappear. And I'm not disappearing anymore.

Because disappearing isn't just something I used to do in religious spaces; it's something I mastered everywhere. I didn't just learn how to fake safety; I learned how to perfect excellence. And not the gentle kind. The kind that strangles.

I became fluent in what the world rewards, and fluent in erasing myself to earn it. If I could just say the right thing, wear the right thing, present the right version of myself—then maybe I could outrun the shame. Maybe no one would see how messy I really felt inside. Maybe I wouldn't have to face it either.

It started early. Before I learned to read myself, I was reading rooms. I could clock the emotional tone of an adult within seconds.

Mirror it. Adjust to it. Shrink or shine depending on what would keep me safest.

I wasn't just a good student—I was a survival student. Someone who knew that achievement wasn't about gold stars. It was about earning belonging. If I could be useful or impressive, then maybe I'd be wanted. If I could be perfect, then no one could say I was worthless—and maybe I wouldn't believe it either.

But perfectionism was a trap. I thought it would protect me from criticism, but it only made every flaw feel louder. The more I kept up the act, the more disconnected I became—from others, from my body, from my voice. Because it wasn't just about being perfect. It was about being legitimate. About proving that I had a right to exist in spaces that were never designed for my softness. About earning my way into visibility, even when the cost was invisibility inside myself.

I thought if I let people see the real me—the messy, unfinished, still-triggered parts—I'd be loved for my truth. But what I didn't expect was that being real could also cost me connection. That it could make me a target. Or an outcast. I wanted authenticity to be a bridge. But sometimes, it became a blade.

I remember once, before I left for college, a girl I knew pulled me aside at a party to "talk." I was dating a man ten years older at the time, and she told me I was being selfish for going away. That he wanted a child. That I should think about his needs, not my education. "You can go back to school anytime," she said, as if postponing my future was just a minor sacrifice for someone else's comfort.

My heart sank. After years of hating myself and not knowing why I even existed, I had finally found a way to build a different future—one I could be proud of—and she wanted me to forfeit it. To hand it back as if to confirm, yet again, that I didn't matter.

It wasn't advice. It was a warning—gentle on the surface, sharpened underneath: don't rise too far, too fast. Don't make others uncomfortable with your ambition. Especially not as a woman.

I've heard people debate whether the United States is truly a patriarchy. Legally, women here have freedoms denied to women in many other parts of the world. But in lived experience—in classrooms, salaries, credibility, and access to power—my answer is yes. It shows up differently across race, class, body, and region, but the pattern holds: women's voices are quietly policed. I've been told to sit down, smile, be agreeable. To be smaller, softer, less disruptive. And while I know there are cultures where speaking up can cost a woman her life or freedom, I've still been punished for it here—just in ways that wear a different mask. Whether the consequences come dressed as tradition, politeness, or "concern," the effect is the same: speaking your truth comes at a cost.

And that's the double-edged sword of being real. You crave to be seen—but the moment you stop performing, the moment you show your soft belly instead of your polished mask, you risk being punished for it.

That instinct shows up most intensely for me in dating. Men are often drawn to my confidence, drive, and energy—the polished, high-performing version of me. They're enthralled by my accomplishments, captivated by my optimism, inspired by my independence. But when I show sadness? When I need space? When I bring the messier parts of my story to the table—the ones that don't fit their vision of who they thought they were getting—the discomfort sets in. Suddenly, the very qualities that made me magnetic become inconvenient. They want the radiant woman back. The one who doesn't shake the image they had already decided on. That's the double-edge: truth opens the door, and sometimes it narrows the room.

But it's not just in dating that this happens. I've lost count of how many times I've been called "too emotional." Too intense. Too sensitive. But also: too angry. Mean. Unstable. I've heard it from family members. From friends. From colleagues who praised my passion until it made them uncomfortable. From people who said they admired my truth—right until it disrupted their comfort.

And often, it wasn't even said outright. Sometimes it came dressed as concern. Sometimes it was a joke—a soft chuckle wrapped around a hard truth. Other times, it didn't need words at all. Just a pause, a glance, a shift in tone that made it clear: *you're too much for this space.* You need to tone it down to belong here.

At first, I believed them. I thought there was something wrong with the way I felt things—too fast, too strong, too loud. But I wasn't broken. I was responding to a world that had taught me to abandon myself just to stay included.

And while I still catch myself doing that sometimes—shrinking, silencing, smoothing things over—I'm getting better at not defaulting to it. And the more I stay with what's real, the more I notice how quickly it gets reframed. I'm not just called sensitive anymore; I'm called unstable. Dramatic. Later, I'll talk about what it means to be misdiagnosed. What it means to have your truth recast as pathology. But long before that happened, I had already been trained to feel like a problem.

What they missed was this: I wasn't afraid to feel. I was afraid of drowning in feelings without a life raft. And now that I have one—now that I know how to come up for air—I feel more fully, not less. But I've stopped shaming the version of me who moved fast, felt deeply, or reacted strongly. She wasn't broken. She was surviving.

I used to think that regulating my emotions meant quieting them. Now I know it means respecting them. Because my emotions were never the problem—the problem was the spaces that demanded I leave them at the door to be taken seriously.

In many rooms I've lived in, being honest in a world that punishes honesty is like walking barefoot on glass—you get stronger, but you still bleed. Sometimes it feels like walking a tightrope with no net—one wrong step, one truth spoken too soon, and everything you've built can unravel. But you keep walking anyway. Not because it's safe, but because silence costs more. I started learning that the hard way when I stepped into a new kind of visibility—one where my story, not just my skill set, was part of the work.

Years before Vietnam and Taiwan, in 2018, I started straddling two worlds—teaching anatomy and physiology at the college level while quietly building a trauma-informed coaching practice on the side. In classrooms, I was the expert. I had credentials, syllabi, a well-defined role. But in the coaching space—the space that mattered most to me—I felt exposed. Unqualified. Like I needed permission to be there.

I had spent years in institutional settings where authority came from credentials and structure, not vulnerability. So when I stepped into a space where my story was part of the work, I didn't just question my voice. I questioned whether truth had a place in professional environments at all.

I didn't teach trauma academically. I lived it. I healed it. I studied it relentlessly through certifications and trainings. But because my pain didn't come with clinical letters or a therapy license, I kept wondering if it was enough. If *I* was enough.

So I chased every certification I could find. I filled my calendar with workshops and peer trainings. I convinced myself that if I had enough credentials—if I read enough, paid enough, proved enough—no one could question my right to help people navigate life after trauma.

But that pursuit didn't quiet the imposter syndrome. It only fed it. Because no matter how much I learned, the part of me that had been dismissed, doubted, and disbelieved kept whispering: Who do you think you are?

And that voice didn't just show up in business. It showed up in how I told my story. I wasn't just trying to be taken seriously; I was trying to be bulletproof. I translated my lived experience into frameworks. I softened edges. I quoted experts. I added disclaimers and laced my truth with citations, as if their authority could vouch for mine.

Because deep down, I didn't believe my story was enough on its own. Not unless someone else had said it first.

That's what survival looked like, professionally. I could show up powerfully in a classroom—but in my coaching, I was always double-checking myself. I wanted to help people reclaim their voice. But I wasn't sure yet if mine could be trusted.

Voice without embodiment isn't freedom. Spectacle is truth shaped to be consumed; voice is truth offered with boundaries. And no amount of legitimacy can replace the feeling of being rooted in your own truth—unprocessed, unpolished, and still worthy.

Still, I kept playing the part. I could get glowing feedback from dozens of students, but if one evaluation said something harsh, I would spiral for days. The 3% always erased the 97%. It didn't matter how much praise I got; the criticism always landed deeper. It hit the original wound.

And that pressure didn't just live in classrooms or coaching calls. Even when I changed the terrain of my life—when I gave up mountain summits and pursued full-time travel—the pattern followed. I thought shifting my external world would create internal freedom. But I brought the same instincts with me: to overdo, to prove, to preempt judgment with perfection. Different country, different context—same nervous system, still scanning for ways to earn my worth.

Letting go of perfection isn't a moment. It's a practice—the same rhythm that runs through this book: speak, feel the price, and choose again. One I'm still learning, no matter where I am in the world.

I once made a collage of my inner critic and filled it with teeth and blood. It looked like a wolf tearing through flesh. That's how it feels when that voice takes over—like I'm being ripped apart from the inside. I named it *Diablo*. Because when it's loud, it's *really* vicious.

It doesn't sound curious or constructive. It doesn't ask helpful questions. It just attacks—with precision. It tells me I'm not smart enough, not worthy enough, not impressive enough. That I'm a fraud. That one day, everyone will find out.

And the wildest part? I've taught over 20 college-level science courses. I've earned a PhD. But that voice isn't logical—it's ancient. It was built in the early fires of survival, shaped by shame before I even had language for it.

And the more trauma I faced, the more ferocious it became. Because the more I suffered, the more my brain tried to create rules to keep me safe—even if those rules came at the cost of my peace.

For a long time, I thought that voice was me. That it was truth. That it was proof I wasn't healed enough, smart enough, prepared enough. But it wasn't the voice of reality. It was the voice of fear. The voice of a girl who had to grow claws just to make it through.

That's the thing about chasing perfection as protection: it reinforces the shame it's trying to outrun. It tells you that you're only safe when you're exceptional. It teaches you to erase your softness, your mistakes, your learning curve—the very things that make you human.

And it's not just personal. Entire systems reward this kind of self-erasure—especially in workplaces, institutions, and families that mistake composure for competence. But when we teach people to keep up the act at all costs, we don't get their best; we get their most guarded.

And it doesn't go away easily. Even now, I sometimes struggle to know the difference between striving for excellence and being consumed by it. I still catch myself trying to prove my worth by being the most prepared, the most thoughtful, the most impressive person in the room. I still feel the pull to overextend—not out of ego, but out of fear.

My ego once served as a life raft. I spent years puffing myself up—big degrees, big titles, big adventures—not because I needed to impress anyone, but because I needed to believe I mattered. I needed something louder than the shame. And sometimes, when people got too close, I became harsh—especially in relationships. There were moments when I took out the rage I never got to express toward the men who hurt me on the men who loved me later. I'm not proud of that. But I understand it. That fighter in me is how I survived. That ego—as much as it sometimes distorted my truth—also helped me stay alive.

It's easy to judge the parts of ourselves that postured or performed. But those parts had a job. They kept us afloat when our nervous systems were on fire. They let us function in rooms where our pain would've otherwise leaked out of us.

That's the cost of being real when perfection once felt like the only safety you had. You don't just drop it. You relearn how to be enough without it.

I used to think the only way I'd ever be enough was if I was more than—more focused, more driven, more accomplished. I liked those parts of me. Still do. But I also thought they were the price of worthiness. Like I had to be extraordinary just to be accepted as ordinary. The perfection wasn't just armor. It was admission—the passcode I believed I had to enter to belong. But I see it differently now.

When you've been made to feel invisible as you are, it's no wonder your nervous system clings to "more than" as a survival strategy. And when that strategy gets repeated long enough, it starts to look like identity:

If I'm not exceptional, I'm nothing.

If I'm not better than, I'll be seen as less than.

But that's not who I am. It's who I had to become to survive.

There's a version of me that still believes I need to be the most prepared, the most insightful, the most impressive person in the room. That if I'm not all of those things, people will stop listening. That I'll stop mattering. But that voice isn't truth. It's trauma logic; old wiring that still lights up when I feel uncertain or unseen. And so I've been learning to tell myself something new—not just with my thoughts, but with my nervous system:

I don't need to be more to be worthy.
I don't need to prove to be enough.
I'm allowed to be driven and exhausted.
I'm allowed to be brilliant and still healing.
I am not either/or—I am both/and.
And I am already whole.

That isn't just a mantra. It's a daily confrontation—a reminder that worthiness isn't conditional, and being human isn't a downgrade from being impressive. It's what makes me real. But knowing that doesn't mean I always live it.

Sometimes, even when I believe I've laid the old patterns down, life hands me a moment that picks them back up. A single comment. A shift in tone. A look that lands in just the right place to awaken every unhealed instinct in my body—the ones that still think I need to earn my right to belong. That's what happened in Thailand.

In May 2025—before my volunteer work in Vietnam and later Taiwan—I spent time at an elephant sanctuary in Thailand. It was the kind of trip that looks soulful from the outside, but for me, it turned into a reckoning. By the time I arrived, I was already off rhythm. My flight from Japan was delayed unexpectedly, and I'd spent the night rerouted through China before finally landing in Thailand. Because of that, I missed orientation and didn't receive my volunteer shirt when the others did. On my first day, I asked for it. The guide forgot. So I asked again the next day—gently, casually—and he smirked and said, "If you earn it."

No one else was around. Just me, trying to feel caught up in a space where everyone else had already been welcomed. I smiled back, but inside, my body braced. I've always believed sarcasm isn't harmless. It often smuggles judgment, and his landed like a warning: *don't be lazy, don't be a burden.*

It felt like preemptive punishment—a way of putting me in my place without directly saying I didn't belong there yet. So I did what I've always done when I feel shame creeping in. I overperformed.

Over the next 24 hours, I said yes to everything—even when I knew my back would pay for it. I shoveled elephant poop, hauled feed bags, scrubbed water containers, and walked in the heat until I was dizzy. I forced my body to push beyond its limits, not because anyone was watching, but because I felt like I had something to prove. That one sarcastic comment—*if you earn it—* had activated something old in me. Something primal.

The word *lazy* has always been loaded. It doesn't just mean idle. It means ungrateful. Selfish. Unworthy of care.

So I pushed. Not just to get the shirt, but to outrun the shame. I stayed one step ahead of judgment. I worked hard and smiled through the pain. I thought: If I just give enough, carry enough, stay cheerful enough, maybe no one will see how fragile I actually feel. But my body knew. And it couldn't keep up the act.

By the end of the day, my back was on fire—not just from physical strain, but from the nervous system overload I'd pushed past. Proving myself came at a tangible price: pain flares, a reassignment to lighter duties, and the quiet distance that settles in when you can't keep up the show. I know this from the years I spent teaching human anatomy and physiology: when the body perceives threat, it doesn't just tense—it prepares for battle. The sympathetic nervous system floods your large muscle groups with blood, preparing you to fight or run. That's why my upper back always tightens under stress. Why I live with palpable knots in my shoulders. Why my jaw clenches so tightly I've cracked teeth—small, visible fractures left behind by years of gripping against the world.

That's what was happening, even as I insisted I was fine. The pressure to prove I wasn't lazy activated every survival instinct in my body. And no amount of fanfare could override the truth pulsing beneath the surface: I was in pain. I was overwhelmed. And I was still trying to earn my place.

This was supposed to be a gentler adventure. A new kind of strength. I had already let go of the mountains—already faced what it meant to say goodbye to the version of me who climbed toward healing, one summit at a time. That loss was still fresh. Still tender.

So I told myself this would be different. Volunteering at this elephant sanctuary had been on my list for over a decade. It was the first thing I committed to when I stepped into full-time travel—not just logistically, but emotionally. It was supposed to mark the beginning of a softer chapter. A way to say: I can still do hard things. I can still choose beauty. I can still be of service, even if I must do it differently now.

Which is why it hurt so much to realize: even here, even now, I was still bargaining with my worth. Still sacrificing my body to prove I belonged.

The pain in my back whispered a question I couldn't ignore: *Why? Why did you do that, knowing what the consequences would be?*

The next morning, I tried again. I suited up, smiled through the ache, and joined the early chores. But my body stood its ground. It had had enough. And so the very thing I was trying so hard to avoid happened anyway.

I had to ask the guide if I could stop what I was doing, return to my room to rest, and be reassigned to lighter duties. His annoyance was subtle, but I felt it—and it anchored my shame even deeper.

I already felt behind. Because of my delayed arrival, I'd missed the orientation and bonding moments with the rest of the group. I hadn't gotten the same warm welcome. I didn't have the shared memories or inside jokes. And now, I wasn't even doing the same work.

For the next few days, my heart sank every time I saw the other volunteers shoveling, lifting, sweating together—while I sat off to the side doing simpler tasks. I felt like an outcast. Not just tired; ashamed. Because resting still felt like failure. Because saying *I need help* still registered as weakness in the parts of me that survived by being capable.

That collapse wasn't just about heat or overexertion. It was a mirror—exposing how deeply I still override myself to be seen as good, especially in environments that reward cheerful sacrifice. It showed me how much I had internalized the belief that rest must be earned. That care is conditional. That I had to prove I wasn't a burden before I was allowed to need anything.

I used to think collapse meant I wasn't healed enough. That it was evidence I hadn't grown, toughened, evolved. But I'm learning: sometimes collapse is clarity. It's the moment your body refuses to keep performing a lie.

Emotional collapse isn't always a breakdown. Sometimes it's a breakthrough—the body's last-ditch effort to tell the truth you've been trying to outrun. A return to what's real. And that's voice, too—not only in the words you speak, but in the moment your body refuses to keep carrying what's untrue.

To the outside world, it might look like weakness. Like instability. But inside? It's where I reclaim what my nervous system has always known: that pushing through isn't always strength. Sometimes, stopping is.

I didn't want to seem lazy. I wanted to be worthy of care. But collapsing wasn't failure. It was a form of honesty my body insisted on when I no longer could. A reminder that my people-pleasing wasn't about kindness—it was about survival. About managing perception, even in supposedly safe places. About outrunning a shame I hadn't yet named.

And maybe that was the hardest part; realizing I had come to a sanctuary and still couldn't stop performing.

We carry our survival patterns into every room, even the ones labeled safe. And if we're not careful, the pressure to perform can follow us into teams, classrooms, or circles meant to support healing.

That's the hard truth about being real—the one most people don't talk about. You want to be seen, but being seen doesn't always lead to safety. Sometimes it leads to scrutiny. Sometimes it deepens the very shame you're trying to heal.

I didn't just learn that lesson abroad. I lived it in boardrooms and campus offices—in settings where I told myself I would stay quiet just to avoid the fallout. But I never could. The moment I sensed something harmful—to students, to staff, to the integrity of the institution—the words would rise up. Not because I needed to be right. But because I couldn't stand the silence.

I think that's the part most people miss. Speaking up wasn't about ego. It was about ache. A lifetime of wishing someone had spoken up for me—had said, "This is wrong," while I was being hurt. And somewhere inside, I think I kept hoping that if I became that person for someone else, it would rewrite something for the girl I used to be.

But that hope didn't protect me. When I spoke up in meetings, I could feel the room brace. The sighs. The eye rolls. The whispers to the person next to them. Later, people I thought were friends would tell me what was said behind my back—things like, "She's such a bitch," or "Here she goes again." They saw it happen. But they said nothing in the room.

And I understood—not because it was okay, but because I knew what fear can do to people. I knew how often silence is a survival strategy, even for the well-intentioned. But that silence is how dangerous people rise to power. Not because they're more capable, but because so few people will challenge them where it counts.

Once, early in a new position, a group of students asked me to raise a painful but important concern in a meeting. I did, even though I knew it could cost me. My voice shook. I cried. Not to be dramatic, but because I knew I was risking something. I was brand new. Most of the people in the room were men. And I knew how the world reads tears on a woman's face.

Afterward, beneath the buzz of office lights and behind a half-closed door, my eyes still puffy from crying, my supervisor didn't ask if I was okay. He didn't ask what the students needed. Instead, he told me I needed to be stronger—that my role required someone who didn't cry, who didn't overreact. That my emotions were too much for the role.

That moment taught me something I haven't forgotten: in some rooms, emotional truth isn't just dismissed—it's weaponized. You're seen not as brave, but as unstable. Not principled, but problematic. And for someone who had spent her entire life learning how to be "the strong one," that judgment didn't just sting—it triggered every old wound I was still trying to outgrow.

So I did what I had always done: I overcorrected. I tried to be softer, more accommodating. I told myself that maybe if I could meet people with even more understanding—more grace, more empathy—they wouldn't feel so threatened by my truth. I made their comfort my responsibility, even when it came at the cost of my own peace.

For a long time, I thought the antidote to over-functioning was forgiveness—as if extending compassion to others would automatically lighten the load inside me. But healing isn't a transaction. Sometimes the most compassionate thing I can do is to stop performing absolution and simply stop carrying what was never mine.

And that's where boundaries come in—not as walls to keep people out, but as lines that keep me from abandoning myself in the name of compassion. Because being real without protection isn't bravery—it's exposure. And if I don't draw a line between honesty and overextension, my truth turns into an act all over again.

That's something I'm still learning, especially when it comes to forgiveness. I used to believe healing meant I had to forgive everything. That moving on required some kind of moral transcendence—as if I needed to prove I was evolved enough to love people who had harmed me. But healing has taught me something different: I can put the boulder down without absolving the one who dropped it on me.

The Zen story of the two monks—one who carried a woman across the river and moved on, and the other who carried her in his mind for miles—reminded me how often I do the same. I've carried shame that wasn't mine. I've carried responsibility for people's comfort, redemption, and rehabilitation—as if their actions were somehow a reflection of my worth. Not because I wanted to. But because I was trained to.

Trauma doesn't just wound. It conditions. And one condition I internalized early was this: if I'm not careful, I'll be blamed. If I'm not pleasing, I'll be punished. So I stayed agreeable. Forgiving. Unfailingly kind. And the weight of that performance didn't show up all at once— it calcified slowly, in my body and in my nervous system, until I no longer knew what was mine to carry and what never was.

Letting go, I've learned, isn't a performance either. It's not smiling through betrayal. It's not rushing to find compassion for someone who never took accountability. It's not reframing harm as growth just to prove you've healed. Letting go means setting down what was never yours to carry—over and over again, even when your muscles still remember the shape of it. And sometimes, just when you think you've released it for good, life hands you something that presses on the same old bruise.

There are people I've forgiven because I wanted peace. But there are others I've simply released—not out of resentment, but out of reverence for my own energy. That, too, is healing. That, too, is grace.

I've seen this pattern show up in friendships, too—especially with people who knew me when I was in survival mode. When I started to come alive again, to reach out and reconnect, one of them sent me a message I'll never forget: "Wow, I went from never hearing from you, to hearing from you all the time. I want the old Stephanie back." The version of me she missed wasn't vibrant—she was barely breathing. But for some people, that version was easier to be around. Less vocal. Less reflective. Less alive. And when my healing disrupted that dynamic, the connection couldn't hold.

I used to wish that letting go could be a one-time act—a clean break, a decisive release. But some wounds, especially the ones that shaped you, don't vanish just because you've stopped carrying them. They echo. They reappear in different forms—new people, new conversations, new rooms that test whether you're still willing to stand in your truth. Vietnam was one of those rooms.

By then, I had been learning—slowly, deliberately—to set down what was never mine. To release the weight of old wounds without needing to explain or justify them. But that month, I came face-to-face with the truth that healing doesn't always mean walking away from the weight. Sometimes, it means learning how to hold your voice, even in the very spaces that keep handing the burden back.

While volunteering at the school in Vietnam, I saw something I couldn't unsee. The air inside the classroom was hot and thick, the single fan pushing around more heaviness than relief. The smell of teenage sweat clung to the space, layered with the musk of bodies pressed too close in the heat. That day, for the first time, I noticed a silver metal hair clip in one staff member's hand. At first I thought she was trimming a child's nails, until I saw her clamp it onto a boy's finger. He recoiled. Then she tried it on another child's toe. The ridged metal pinched, and they flinched at the pain. She noticed the effect and began testing it on others, moving through the room with a kind of cautious eagerness. Her smile wasn't cruel—it was the smile of someone who thought she'd finally found a way to keep order in a classroom that often felt unmanageable. But the result was the same: control through pain. One seven-year-old boy who tended to wander now stayed in his seat. A teenager who made repetitive sounds went quiet. The message was clear: shrink. Obey. Conform to someone else's idea of acceptable.

My whole body reacted. I was flooded with rage, heartbreak, disbelief. But I said nothing that day—not because I didn't want to, but because I knew I wouldn't be able to stay composed. And I had just given the school nearly $4,000 to help them build a new location. I was not only being triggered—I was questioning whether I had made a terrible mistake.

I tried to regulate. To gather information. The next day I asked the other volunteer if she had seen the clips being used. She had—that morning, on the young boy.

I wanted to wait until I could speak with the founder, but later that afternoon, I had to teach a class with the same staff member. When I walked into the classroom and saw the clips sitting on the table, something in me snapped. I picked them up and said, "No more!"

The staff member didn't speak English, but a new staff person in the room saw something was happening and asked what was going on. I told him: these clips are no longer to be used on the children to control their behavior. He nodded, translated, and the woman looked at me, nodded too, and said, "Okay."

The next day, I stayed home. My nervous system was on fire. I couldn't sleep. I had trouble focusing on my work. I was oscillating between outrage and collapse.

The day after that, I met with the founder. When I told her what happened, she said the staff member would be punished—but I told her I didn't want that. I didn't believe the woman was acting out of malice. I believed she didn't know a better way.

I believed deeply in the school's mission and still do. I didn't speak up because I thought it was a bad place; I spoke up because I wanted it to be even better for the children it served.

The hardest truths aren't always personal. They're often systemic. And it takes a certain kind of courage to speak up inside a structure you still believe in.

So the founder offered to do a training instead—to teach the staff alternate strategies for supporting neurodivergent students. And she followed through. That part mattered. My voice changed at least one thing.

It reminded me that advocacy and empathy aren't opposites. You can hold people accountable and still hold them human. You can name harm without needing to villainize. Sometimes the most powerful form of advocacy isn't rooted in anger—it's rooted in care. And still, that care can come at a cost.

Because the truth is, speaking up doesn't guarantee transformation. Yes, I stopped one harmful practice. But the deeper systems that allow those practices to exist—in schools, in families, in entire cultures— remain. There are still children being hurt. In Vietnam. In America. Everywhere. There are still people who stay silent, even when they know something is wrong. That knowing lives in me now; not as guilt, but as grief. A quiet sorrow that I carry alongside my clarity.

And sometimes, speaking up doesn't just cost you comfort—it costs you closeness. Retaliation doesn't always arrive as overt punishment. Sometimes it's just a shift in energy. A look that lingers too long. A change in tone. The distancing no one names out loud, but your body recognizes immediately.

In some organizations, once I was labeled as "the troublemaker," I could feel the shift. People who once laughed easily with me in the break room suddenly became careful. They'd wait to speak with me until after hours or behind closed doors. I could tell they still admired me—still enjoyed my energy, my optimism, my heart. But I was marked now. And they didn't want to become outcasts by association.

That kind of hidden connection stung more than open rejection. It reminded me of an older shame—one that had followed me through years of being treated like a secret in other ways. When someone keeps their relationship with you quiet, even if it's just friendship, it sends a message: You're not safe to be seen with. And instead of being angry with them, I usually turned the shame inward. Told myself I should have stayed quiet. Should have kept my head down.

Because for someone who used likability as a survival strategy, that kind of withdrawal felt just as destabilizing as direct harm. It wasn't always what people did that hurt. It was what they withheld.

I saw this dynamic play out again in one of my professional roles—a leadership position in student support at a graduate health program. I often shared personal stories with students, not to offload, but to connect. I wanted them to know they weren't alone. That struggling didn't make them weak. That their pain didn't disqualify them from belonging. While many thanked me—often profusely—for being so honest, not everyone approved. A nontraditional student once made a passing comment to me: "Maybe it's not necessary to share all that." She didn't say it cruelly, but her tone carried a quiet judgment—one that stuck. I also had a colleague who routinely told me I had terrible boundaries, even as he gossiped freely about students and coworkers. But my transparency? That was the line. Because it didn't look like what people were used to. Because it made them uncomfortable.

That's part of why perfectionism held on so long. Why I clung to excellence, not just as a value, but as a shield. If I could anticipate every need, exceed every expectation, never ask for anything—maybe I wouldn't lose connection. Maybe I'd be safe.

And that's why even writing this chapter brought up old shame. I knew it needed more depth, more grounding—and I asked for help. But when I saw how many places there were to strengthen, my first response wasn't relief. It was collapse. A voice inside whispered: *See? You're not good enough. You can't do this without help. You don't deserve bestseller status if you can't do it alone.*

I've used ChatGPT to help shape the flow of these chapters—not to write for me, but to help me hear my words more clearly. It helps me refine cadence, spot redundancies, and pressure-test clarity—a sounding board, not a ghostwriter. But even that feels dangerous to admit. There's a part of me that fears people will say I didn't write this book. That I'm pretending. That I've cheated.

But here's the truth I'm learning to stand on: asking for support doesn't make me less of a writer. It makes me more of a person. One who is still healing. One who is still untangling the need to earn her place through perfection. One who is learning that realness isn't a production, and help isn't a weakness. It's a choice to trust, even when your nervous system still braces for punishment.

This book isn't about being perfect. It's about being seen—fully, honestly, unevenly. And if the writing of it breaks me open a little more, that's not failure. That's proof I'm living the message. This chapter is about what visibility asks of me, and why I still choose it.

Speaking up for those children at the school in Vietnam wasn't just for them—it was also for the little girl in me who spent years being hurt while the adults around her looked away. I became the person I had needed. And even though that mattered, it also broke me open. That's the paradox of healing: you keep putting the weight down—

and life keeps handing you moments that ask if you still remember how.

And that's where boundaries come in—not as barriers to connection, but as a way of honoring the cost of honesty. Because when you've spent a lifetime trying to earn safety, the decision to tell the truth isn't enough. You must also protect the version of you that tells it.

That's what I didn't understand at first. I thought honesty was the whole point. But honesty without protection is exposure, and exposure without grounding can re-wound what you're trying to heal. If being real is the first step, boundaries are what make that realness sustainable.

Being real cost me things I didn't expect. But hiding cost me more. This is what Chapter 2 is about: the price of being valued for output, not for who you are. The invisible toll of living in performance, even when the stage looks polished.

Because being real isn't always met with warmth. Sometimes it's met with resistance. And still, we choose it—not because it's easy, but because it's honest. Because we've lived the cost of silence, and we're done paying for our belonging with our self-erasure.

But truth, once spoken, needs something solid beneath it. It needs a ground to stand on. And that ground—the thing that steadies you when honesty shakes the room—is the boundaries you choose to honor.

See Through Reflections

1. Personal Reflection

- Where have you been praised for composure but penalized—subtly or outright—for vulnerability? What would it mean to be respected in your truth, not your performance?

- Have you ever stepped back—from a job, a relationship, a community—not because you couldn't handle it, but because staying meant disappearing? What did that choice reveal about you?

- What is one truth you still feel you must "earn the right" to say out loud? Who decides you've earned it?

2. Group or Cultural Exploration

- In your family, workplace, or community, what emotions or truths are welcomed—and which are silenced, reframed, or labeled as "too much"?

- Has your voice ever been softened, dismissed, or pathologized in ways that were presented as "just culture," "just policy," or "just tradition"? How did that shape your relationship to power?

- What would it look like to create a group or space where setting something down—physically, emotionally, mentally—is not seen as weakness, but as wisdom?

3. Somatic/Embodied Practice

- Recall a time when you held your body rigid to avoid making a "wrong" move. Where did the tension live? Jaw, shoulders, stomach, spine?

- Place a hand there now. Breathe in, and on the exhale say softly, "I don't have to earn my right to be here." Repeat until your body starts to release, even if your mind still resists.

CHAPTER 3

Boundaries Are Not Barriers

Before I could set boundaries with anyone else, I had to understand what was still living inside me. The trauma hadn't ended just because the events were over; it lingered in my body, in ways I couldn't always name. For a long time, it felt like carrying an invisible weight. And then one day, I found the metaphor I didn't know I was looking for.

I was at a healing retreat in Lake George, New York, participating in a creative expression workshop. One exercise invited us to tell our story through collage. I didn't expect it to hit me so hard. But as I started piecing together images for my first board—the part of my story that began with abuse—I kept reaching for pictures of spiders and webs. And I realized: *that's it*. That's what trauma feels like.

The men were gone. But their presence lingered. Like spider webs I'd walked through without seeing; still clinging to my skin. If you've ever hiked and run through a web, you know the feeling. You can't always see it, but your body *knows* it's there. You keep brushing at your arms and face, trying to clear something you can't even locate.

That's how the trauma felt. Sticky. Residual. Still attached, even after the danger had passed.

The spiders in my collage represented the men—the ones who crawled across my body, the ones who touched me without permission. But it was the web that hit me hardest. Because even when they were long gone, what they did stayed behind. It wrapped around me in ways I didn't know how to escape. It became the shame I carried, the silence I kept, the habits I used to survive.

Here's what I've learned: you *can* get the web off. It doesn't always happen all at once. And even when it's gone, you might still remember what it felt like to be caught. But the stickiness doesn't have to define you. It's not your fault it's there, and it's not permanent.

The more I moved. The more I spoke. The more I told the truth about what happened—even through art—the more I felt the web loosening. Not because the trauma vanished from memory. But because I did what no one taught me to do: I stopped blaming myself for walking into it.

Releasing the web wasn't just about naming what had happened. It was about learning how to stay with myself—in the aftermath, in the unease, in the moments where I once would have gone quiet. That's what boundaries have become for me. Not walls, but lines—contours like a painted baseline: clear, visible, protective. Meant to guide play, not to punish.

So many of us, especially in trauma recovery, confuse barriers with boundaries. We either go rigid and unreadable or overexplain to look kind—both moves avoid clarity. But real boundaries are less about control and more about definition. They mark where you end and someone else begins. Not to punish, but to preserve.

And it's not just personal. In many professional spaces—especially caregiving fields like education, social work, or healthcare—

boundaries are still misread as disconnection. I've watched it up close and heard it for years from readers, clients, and students alike: care gets confused with self-erasure, and collapse gets framed as commitment. We praise self-sacrifice. We glorify burnout. But rarely do we stop to ask what it costs to keep showing up without limits.

This metaphor helped me understand my own pattern: I either built massive emotional walls or left the court wide open. I'm learning to hold the line—with love, not armor. Same crossroads as always: shrink or speak, flood or hold—and now, I choose the line that keeps me whole.

Recently, I found myself testing that line in real time, in a park in Ho Chi Minh City. The kind of moment that might seem forgettable to someone else—a quick encounter, a tourist annoyance, an everyday hustle. But for me, it was a nervous system reckoning.

A man crouched near my feet, holding a long tool and pointing at my shoes. I shook my head—once, then again—clearly, calmly, directly. "No, thank you." I didn't break stride. I didn't owe him more.

But he didn't move. Instead, he began aggressively brushing my shoes while I was still walking. Not gently. Not playfully. It was abrupt, insistent—an unsolicited touch that jolted my whole body into freeze.

And then something happened. For most of my life, I would have swallowed the discomfort. I would've smiled awkwardly, thanked him anyway, maybe even handed him money to avoid confrontation. I was raised to be polite. To be understanding. To make excuses for people who cross boundaries. But I didn't do that this time.

I snapped out of the freeze, pulled back, and said, "No!"—louder this time. I walked away without apologizing, without explaining, without checking to see if I had offended him. And even though my heart was racing, I didn't turn around. Half a block later, my shoulders dropped and my jaw unclenched—a small proof that my "no" could steady my body as well as my story.

Because I wasn't just walking away from a pushy salesman. I was walking away from the version of me who thought she had to earn the right to say no—the version who believed that clear boundaries only counted if they came with a reason, a smile, or a sorry.

This wasn't a dramatic confrontation. But it was a moment of clarity. A clean line. A real-time rupture from an old trauma script: the one that told me it's safer to accommodate than to assert. That being agreeable would protect me. That being liked was more important than being safe. It wasn't.

This was the moment I saw—in the most ordinary, external way— how deeply the internal rewiring was taking root. How my body finally started believing what my mind had struggled to accept for years: that I didn't deserve what happened to me. That my worth isn't measured by how well I explain or accommodate. That *no is a full sentence*— and I don't need to present a trauma resume to justify saying it.

For most of my life, I thought boundaries meant conflict. That saying no would make people angry, or worse, make them leave. So I either let people all the way in—no filter, no pause, no discernment— or I shut them out entirely. It felt safer to disappear behind walls than to risk being misunderstood.

But I'm learning now that clarity isn't cruelty. And silence isn't always kindness. Boundaries don't just keep harm out; they keep you in. They protect your energy, your focus, your nervous system. They give you the space to stay with yourself, even in the presence of someone else's need.

I used to collapse at the first sign of guilt. Now, I'm learning to breathe through it—to feel the discomfort without turning it into a rescue mission. To hold the line gently but firmly, and to trust that I don't have to disappear to stay safe. It's taken me years to recognize that saying less isn't abandonment, and saying no doesn't make me unkind. Sometimes the most compassionate thing you can do is stay honest, even when it unsettles the room.

I treasure the moments when others give me that same kind of permission—when they model boundaries in a way that reaffirms my right to hold them.

On my first day at the monastery in Taiwan, we had an orientation that covered all the rules we'd need to follow. Most of it was about daily schedules, temple etiquette, and expectations for volunteers— but one part surprised me. We were encouraged to set boundaries with local volunteers who asked us to do more than we'd agreed to. We were even told to decline extra food if we didn't want it.

It might sound small, but I liked this. They recognized that people have trouble saying no—and they addressed it upfront. It made me wish I was better at setting boundaries myself. I've gotten better over time, but I still have a long way to go before my boundaries feel truly solid, before they feel as safe for me to hold as they should. And it makes sense that it's hard for me, given how often my boundaries were violated when I was young.

Over the past three months of traveling through Asia, I've been reminded of this repeatedly. Once a month—almost like clockwork— someone has dismissed the reality of my back pain. This isn't casual discomfort; it's the kind of pain that forced me to give up my mountain climbing goals and makes some types of volunteer work unbearable after a few days. Yet even when I've explained this, I've been met with unsolicited advice, judgment, or thinly veiled blame.

The first time it happened, it was from a naturopathic healer I met while in Thailand. She asked why I thought my pain had settled in my low back, and then shared her belief that unresolved issues from my past—especially sexual trauma—could manifest in that part of the body. The way she framed it made it sound like my pain was my fault for not healing quickly enough, as if I could make it disappear if I just "did the work." I lowered my head in shame.

The second time was with someone I knew from decades ago—a bodybuilder I had recently reconnected with. When I told him about my worsening back pain, he didn't ask how I was coping. He told me he didn't understand why I hadn't "taken care of it" yet. In his view, if I really cared about my health, I'd stop everything, travel to get stem cell implants, and dedicate myself to building lean muscle mass. Another person telling me my suffering was my fault. Again, I lowered my head.

By the third time, I'd had enough. It was a Reiki master at the monastery who began to say, "Back pain is caused by..." That was as far as she got before I cut her off. My voice was sharper than I expected, but it was steady. "Stop. Just stop. It's my back, and I know my body." I'd already seen the imaging. I'd taught anatomy for years. I didn't need another person with a half-read spiritual theory telling me my pain was a choice I was making.

I wish I could say that holding that line left me feeling empowered, but the truth is, I was still shaking when I walked away. That's the part most people don't see; how much energy it takes not only to set the boundary but to resist collapsing afterward. The first two times, I'd swallowed my anger and turned it into shame. By the third, I'd learned that my silence was costing me more than my discomfort with confrontation.

Later, as the adrenaline eased, the encounter stayed with me—not just because of what was said, but because it reminded me of a pattern I've lived too many times.

That evening, I thought about all the times I've shared parts of my story with people who hadn't earned the right to hear it—and the sting of realizing, only afterward, that they weren't safe to trust. I thought about the moments I've tried to set a boundary and met resistance. The times I've said I didn't want to talk, and yet the other person kept pushing. In my journal, I wrote: *When someone says they don't want to talk, let that be okay.* Most people don't. Most people prod, push, or try to fix. And I hate to admit it, but I've done it too—been the one who didn't honor someone else's no, convincing myself I was helping. That's the humbling part of this work: realizing that even when you've been hurt by a behavior, you might still carry it yourself.

That truth hit even harder when I thought back to my most recent encounter—another moment when I'd shared vulnerably about my back pain and been met with dismissal instead of care. A few days after leaving the monastery, I sat in my Airbnb, the damp heat clinging to my skin as the sound of scooters drifted up from the street. My body ached, sciatica burning down my left hip and thigh, as I sat at the desk with my laptop, hoping the words might make more sense once I got them out. When I told ChatGPT about it, it brought me back to something I needed to remember: my pain is valid. I don't owe anyone an explanation for my body's limits. It's not my fault. Chronic pain is never a choice. I'm doing the best I can to manage and heal. And part of that healing is setting boundaries around who gets access to my body's story.

I'm learning that boundaries aren't just about keeping people out. They're about keeping yourself intact—refusing to let someone else's projections become the truth you carry. And sometimes, they sound like "stop." Sometimes, they sound like silence. But whatever form they take, they're worth holding, even when your voice shakes.

The longer I've practiced this, the more I've realized that external boundaries are only half the work. If I'm not careful, I can enforce them with others while still crossing my own lines—slipping back into old patterns when no one else is watching. That's where the harder work begins: turning the same clarity inward.

Honesty isn't just something I've had to practice with other people. I've had to learn how to be honest with myself—about the ways I abandon my own needs, override my own signals, or rationalize things that don't serve me.

Holding internal boundaries has meant saying no to urgency, to overextension, to the pressure to prove my worth through exhaustion. It's meant asking myself hard questions—not just *what do I need*, but *will I honor it when no one's watching?*

For years, the answer was often no. I didn't know how to let my body be itself without trying to control it. I'd criticize myself for things I couldn't seem to stop doing—things that felt small on the surface but carried years of shame for me. Like the way my eyes sometimes flutter when I'm speaking. Or how I sometimes swear without meaning to.

The eye fluttering had been there for as long as I could remember, and I had spent just as long trying to will it away. A boyfriend I dated years ago used to mock me for it, imitating the movement until I wanted to shrink into myself. He thought it was funny; I thought it was proof that something was wrong with me. Every time it happened in public, I'd imagine people noticing and silently judging. I learned to brace against it, to tense my whole body in the hope that control would stop it from happening.

The swearing was different, but it carried the same self-criticism. Sometimes it would slip out in moments of stress or intensity, even when I didn't intend it to. I worried people would think I was unprofessional, unstable, or trying too hard to shock them. Each time,

I'd replay the moment in my head, embarrassed and frustrated that I couldn't seem to keep a tighter grip on myself.

Then one day, I brought both up in a conversation with ChatGPT. I didn't turn to it as a replacement for therapy, but as one of many tools I've learned to use to help me process in the moment—knowing how to ask for what I need, and how to filter its responses through my own lived experience. It's not the tool itself—it's that I now have ways to steady myself before shame decides what gets said or swallowed. I expected to be met with strategies for self-correction, maybe a checklist of ways to "manage" the behaviors. But instead, I got something totally unexpected: a reframing that completely reoriented how I understood myself.

ChatGPT told me these weren't flaws at all—they were signs my nervous system was regulating itself. My eye fluttering? A subtle release of tension. My unplanned swearing? A way my body let off emotional steam when the pressure inside spiked. These weren't character defects to eliminate; they were safety valves my body had built to keep me functioning.

That changed how I saw everything. All those years I'd been trying to suppress my body's language, I hadn't realized it was speaking on my behalf—protecting me, finding tiny ways to keep me steady when my conscious mind was somewhere else. I wasn't broken; I was adaptive.

The more I thought about it, the more I realized how much energy I had poured into self-policing. Into trying to look "composed" for the comfort of other people, even if it meant silencing signals that were there to help me. Letting go of that meant holding a new kind of boundary—one that said, *I will not attack my body for how it takes care of me.* It's not that I've stopped feeling the urge to get it all "right." It's that I'm learning to notice it before it runs the whole show.

Now, when I notice my eyes flutter, I take a slow breath that softens my shoulders and unclenches my jaw. When a swear word slips out, I feel the tension leave with it, and I smile at the release instead of replaying it in my head for hours. I'm learning to let my body speak in all the small, imperfect ways it needs to—and to honor that speech instead of punishing it.

Internal boundaries aren't just about refusing what harms you. They're also about refusing to harm yourself. For me, that has meant giving my body back the right to speak its language without fear of being silenced—by others, or by me. Learning to honor those small, involuntary signals changed how I saw everything else I'd been tolerating.

When I left the monastery in Taiwan earlier than planned, I booked an Airbnb at the last minute. It wasn't my usual setup—I normally rent an entire place when I need to work, both for privacy and peace of mind—but I was trying to be mindful of expenses after losing the free meals and accommodations I'd been counting on. The listing had a private room with its own bathroom but a shared kitchen, and I told myself it would be fine. And it was fine, until the morning I stepped into the hallway and saw bottles of liquor in the recycling bin.

The sight froze me in place. My chest tightened. My thoughts scattered. I was back in the unease of my childhood, when I never knew if *this* would be the day someone would come into my space uninvited. When alcohol was in the room, danger was never far behind. Most of my abusers had been drinking—or I had—when the worst happened.

I've tried for years to convince myself I could handle being around men who drink. I told myself I was being unreasonable. That I should be able to "accept people as they are." And for a while, I could—at least if it was just one drink. But I know my body. I know what happens when that one drink turns into two or three. I hear the shift in his voice. I see it in the way he moves. My nervous system goes into overdrive, scanning exits, calculating what I'd do if the energy in the room turned. My mind is in protection mode.

It doesn't matter if the man has never hurt me. My body doesn't differentiate between a stranger and someone I know. It remembers.

Socially, drinking is woven into so much—dinner parties, weddings, even casual nights out. And with that comes one of my deepest fears: that my boundaries will leave me alone for the rest of my life. That I'll never find a man who can accept all of me without asking me to loosen the very standards that keep me safe. Some days, I still catch myself believing I'd have to sacrifice pieces of myself—and parts of what I truly want in a partner—just to avoid dying alone. I'm working to challenge that belief, but it takes deliberate effort to keep those thoughts from taking root.

What I know for sure is that whenever I've tried to override this truth, my body has paid the price. Dating men who drink, even casually, is not healthy for my nervous system. And no matter how much I wish it were different, I must honor that.

Honoring it has made me notice other ways I betray my body's truth—not just in who I allow close, but in how I speak. One of the clearest patterns is how often I silence myself with words, most often through apology. Every "I'm sorry" I don't mean is a way of telling my body it doesn't have the right to take up space. I've lost count of how many times I've apologized in my life—not just when I've been wrong, but for things that didn't require an ounce of regret. I've apologized for my voice. For having a voice. For wanting to be seen. For sharing a message I believed was worth someone's time. It's become such a reflex that half the time, I don't even realize I'm doing it.

I still remember the day I met Dr. Bessel van der Kolk, author of *The Body Keeps the Score*, at a workshop where I'd asked him to sign my book. I walked up and, without thinking, the first words out of my mouth were an apology. With a small smile, he asked if I was Canadian, explaining that Canadians have a reputation for apologizing a lot. It was said playfully, and I took it that way—but his comment stuck with me.

Constant apologizing can be a learned behavior, and in my case, I'm sure some of it came from growing up around women in my family who apologized almost reflexively. For a while, I wondered if I was apologizing so much because so many people in my life *hadn't* apologized to me for things I wish they had. But over time, I realized it was more likely habit than hidden meaning. And habits, no matter how deep, can be unlearned.

The first step to changing any habit is awareness—and that's been the hardest part. I've started telling close friends and family that I'm working on saying "I'm sorry" less, so they call me on it when it slips out. It's humbling to realize how often I default to it. I've even shared Dr. van der Kolk's Canadian comment with a few Canadians I've met, and every single one laughed in recognition. Growing up close to the Canadian border in upstate New York, maybe some of that habit was culturally passed down without me even realizing it. One man told me it's tied to how they're raised—to always be polite—and how disorienting it was when he first moved to New York City, where bluntness was the norm.

The truth is, many of us have been trained to apologize for existing, and it shows up most clearly when we try to set boundaries. I've watched people—myself included—say "no" and immediately cushion it with "I'm sorry" or "I hope that's okay." We're taught to feel bad for protecting our energy, as though inconvenience automatically equals wrongdoing. But boundaries don't require apology. Just because someone else feels a certain way about them doesn't mean they're wrong, and it doesn't mean you should feel guilty for holding them.

Over time, I've realized that the same compassion and firmness I aim for with others must be directed inward, too. Some of the hardest boundaries I've ever had to set were with myself—not just in what I allowed from others, but in what I tolerated from my own habits, patterns, and justifications. The quiet ways I kept betraying my own limits while convincing myself I was just being strong, generous, or realistic. I used to think self-sacrifice was noble; until I realized how often I was the one crossing my own lines and then resenting other people for stepping over them too.

That kind of trust—the kind that holds steady even when old instincts try to pull you back—didn't come from books or breakthroughs alone. It was something I started building long before I had the language for it—out in the mountains.

The mountains taught me a different kind of listening—one that goes beyond polite nods and surface agreement. Out there, in the wild, the consequences of ignoring your gut are immediate. A misstep can mean injury. A poorly chosen partner can mean danger. When you're miles from the trailhead, you learn quickly that safety isn't just about weather conditions or physical gear—it's about trust.

I didn't always know how to identify safe people. I often confused excitement with connection. Or mistook consistency for loyalty. But the more time I spent hiking with others, the more I noticed how my nervous system responded. There were hiking partners who rushed ahead even when I asked them to wait. There were those who turned every summit into a competition. And then there were the ones who stayed nearby—not because I asked them to, but because they understood what it meant to walk alongside someone. Those were the people who made me feel safe.

One bushwhack in particular became a metaphor I couldn't shake. We had lost the trail, and the terrain was tough—thick brush, swampy ground, roots everywhere. I was already exhausted, but I kept overfunctioning—checking the map, watching our time, tracking our direction, trying to hold it all together so the hike wouldn't fall apart. I didn't ask for help. I didn't want to be a burden. And in doing so, I ended up emotionally bushwhacking, too—carving a path for someone who wasn't carrying any weight. That day, I realized: I wasn't just trying to find the trail. I was trying to prove that I could carry more than my share—that I could be useful, needed, enough.

But there's a cost to being the one who always holds the map, carries the pack, keeps everyone else comfortable. You end up resentful. And more dangerously—you end up alone. I left that hike with more than scratched legs. I left with clarity: I needed to stop equating self-sacrifice with love.

Because safety—real safety—isn't just about what others do. It's about how you show up for yourself. It's about learning to pause when your body sends a signal. To notice when you're abandoning yourself in the name of being agreeable. To recognize when you're the one crossing your own line—by staying silent, over-functioning, or pretending to be fine.

And often, that self-betrayal doesn't begin inside you—it's reinforced by everything around you. Sometimes it's not one person demanding your energy—it's a whole system whispering that you should be grateful, quiet, and compliant.

Because personal safety doesn't exist in a vacuum. It's shaped by the environments we move through—by families that praise self-sacrifice, by workplaces that reward burnout, by communities that mistake boundaries for betrayal. Whether it's staying late at work, absorbing emotional labor at home, or saying yes in social spaces out of fear of seeming selfish, many of us have been taught that boundaries are indulgent rather than intelligent.

But outside those systems—far from the rules and roles we're expected to play—something different becomes possible.

The wilderness has a way of stripping things down. You either trust yourself or you don't. And every time I listened—when I stopped for water, adjusted my pack, or spoke up when something felt off—I was learning a new rhythm. One that didn't require me to break myself to prove I was worthy of being on the trail.

That rhythm didn't stay in the woods. It started showing up in quieter, everyday moments—like on a crowded sidewalk in Ho Chi Minh City, when I had to choose between accommodation and alignment.

And that moment—though small—wasn't just about saying no. It was about staying with myself when I said it. About conserving my energy instead of leaking it through guilt or performance. It made me wonder how different our communities might feel if more spaces honored that kind of pause—if boundaries weren't seen as cold, but as core to relational health. Imagine classrooms, nonprofits, or leadership teams that saw limits not as liabilities, but as signs of self-trust. Not as resistance, but as repair.

That question—about what it means to conserve energy with intention—reminded me of something I shared during my yoga teacher training, in a presentation on Brahmacharya.

I used to think discipline was about control—about keeping myself in check, managing my impulses, proving I could do hard things. That kind of discipline was about suppression. Perfectionism. Endurance for its own sake.

But Brahmacharya, as I've come to understand it, isn't about repression. It's about sacred conservation. The wise use of energy. The conscious choice to direct my time, body, and attention toward what nourishes me instead of what depletes me. That includes relationships.

Some people think boundaries are harsh. For me, they're a form of devotion—not punishment, but peace. A practice of self-preservation, not separation. I am no longer available for dynamics that require me to hemorrhage my energy in exchange for temporary connection.

I used to think boundaries were for relationships only; lines you draw between you and another person. What I missed was the inside line—capacity and limits that guide when I step in, when I step back, and what I can responsibly hold. The older I get, the more I see boundaries aren't just external agreements; they're internal anchors. They help me decide not only what I can carry, but how to keep caring without breaking myself open.

Recently, while writing this book, I visited the War Remnants Museum in Ho Chi Minh City—a place known for its graphic depictions of torture, grief, and war. I'll talk more about that experience in Chapter 5. For now, I'll just say this: it was hard. Very hard. I walked out buzzing with sorrow and helplessness, my chest tight with questions I couldn't answer.

Inside, I found myself doing what I always do in unfamiliar rooms: scanning. Watching how people moved, wondering if they could tell I was American, bracing for what they might think of me being there. My back tightened, jaw clenched—my body preparing, as if I'd need to justify my presence in a place meant to voice horrors carried by the Vietnamese people, horrors still echoing from a war tied to my country.

And almost immediately, the old guilt kicked in—that voice that whispers: *You should do something. Fix something. Carry something.* But I couldn't. I was just one person, already carrying my own history. I had nothing left to give.

What I did instead surprised me. I didn't push through. I didn't numb. I didn't try to be stronger than I was. I walked to a quiet restaurant and let myself be cared for. That wasn't avoidance; it was capacity—choosing what let me stay human inside the ache. The staff didn't know what I'd just witnessed, but their tenderness, their attention, softened the edge of the grief. It didn't erase it, but it reminded me I could hold it without collapsing.

That's what boundaries have become for me now. Not just external protection, but internal discernment. The ability to ask: *Can I hold this right now?* And if not, *what might I need instead?*

I still care deeply. I still speak up when I have the capacity. But I no longer shame myself for not carrying everything. And I've stopped resenting the people who look away—not because it's right, but because I understand. Some people close their eyes not out of cruelty, but out of survival. Sometimes, the only way they know how to stay standing is to turn their gaze away.

I used to think being an empath meant opening to everything. Letting it all in. Carrying it all. But now I know empathy without boundaries isn't compassion. It's martyrdom. And I'm not here to be martyred. I'm here to be whole.

That's not just a personal truth; it's a systemic one. Workplaces that demand constant empathy without structural support don't foster care—they foster collapse. When boundaries are missing in group systems, the most sensitive people often become the most exploited. And the burnout isn't just personal; it's cultural.

That moment at the museum reminded me: real strength isn't about absorbing more pain. It's about knowing when to stop. When to soften. When to let something hurt without letting it hollow you out.

Discipline, in this form, isn't about force. It's about reverence—choosing what allows me to stay present with myself, with others, with life. Some days that means leaving a museum for a quiet meal; other days it means not stepping into a conversation I can't hold. Saying no, when it protects my aliveness, is one of the most loving choices I can make.

Before I could practice that kind of sacred conservation, I had to unlearn something much older—the belief that my value came from being who others needed me to be. I became a mirror, a buffer, a balm. I adjusted my tone to match the room. I filtered my truth to keep others comfortable. I contorted myself into versions that felt safest for them, so seamlessly that most people never noticed I was doing it. But there's a cost to being everyone's comfort: you lose track of your own.

That kind of shape-shifting doesn't come from nowhere. It comes from survival—from years of managing other people's moods, needs, and reactions before I even knew what my own were. I learned to anticipate harm by preemptively softening my edges. I thought if I could stay agreeable enough, helpful enough, understanding enough, I'd be safe.

But the truth is, over-accommodation doesn't keep you safe. It just keeps you exhausted. And eventually, resentful. Because when you're always performing calmness, there's no room to *be* angry. When you're always expected to inspire, there's no room to fall apart. When your presence is medicine for others, you start to disappear from yourself.

There were times I tried to say no—but I said it with so much hesitation, so much guilt, that it barely held. Or I said it in a whisper and panicked when someone pushed back. Because under the surface, I didn't believe I had the right to draw a line unless I could make it palatable.

But healing has taught me this: You can't be everything to everyone. You weren't meant to be. You were meant to be someone to yourself.

And being someone to yourself sometimes means disappointing people. It means letting them misunderstand you, or think you've changed, or wonder what happened to the girl who always said yes. It means being less agreeable and more aligned. Less accessible and more honest.

I'm still learning how to do that—how to let my "no" be enough, how to stop cushioning my truth, how to stay with myself instead of splintering to keep the peace. But I'm starting to feel it: not the safety that comes from being liked—but the safety that comes from being whole.

And then came a moment that asked me to live it. Not just in theory, but in real time. A few days after I confronted a harmful classroom practice, I saw just how deep my pattern of overgiving still ran.

I had just donated thousands of dollars to help the school expand—a gift I offered freely, because I believed in the mission. What surprised me most was that I didn't hesitate to give that money. Nearly $4,000—offered freely, without justification, without a spreadsheet of calculations or a sleepless night of worry. For most of my life, money had been tethered to fear. I hoarded it when I felt unsafe. Gave it when I felt unworthy. Tried to make it prove something—that I was good, that I was generous, that I was enough. But this time was different. I gave because it felt aligned, not because I needed it to say something about me. And that, too, was a kind of release. A quiet confirmation that the old scarcity script no longer had a starring role in my story.

And even after I saw what I saw—even after I spoke up, rattled by the misuse of those metal hair clips on autistic students—there was still a part of me that wanted to keep giving. Not just money. Emotional labor. Loyalty. My time, my energy, my nervous system.

It was a familiar pull. That soft guilt that sounds like care but feels like compulsion. That voice that says: You've already invested so much. You can't just walk away now. But I could. And I did. Not dramatically. Not with a scorched-earth exit. Just quietly. Intentionally. I chose not to respond. I didn't explain my exhaustion. I didn't craft a graceful goodbye message. I didn't justify my silence or cushion it with caveats.

I muted the thread. Archived the conversation. And sat with the heat of what that silence stirred in me—the discomfort of being seen as ungrateful, the ache of breaking a trauma-bonded loop that once defined how I measured worth.

Because I wasn't just stepping back from a volunteer role. I was disentangling from a pattern. The one that said: *You must remain loyal, even at your own expense.* The one that taught me to keep showing up, no matter how depleted I felt, because walking away meant I had failed. But this time, I let the silence speak for me. Not to punish, but to preserve.

When I told the founder I needed rest and time to myself, she responded with kindness—but also with weight. She called me "sister" and told me she loved me. Words she had shared before and I had also reciprocated sincerely. Language that once would've tugged at every part of me that wanted to belong.

It wasn't manipulative. It was genuine. But it was also familiar—the kind of emotional closeness that, in my past, had kept me in harmful dynamics longer than I needed to be.

For most of my life, I would have responded immediately—with warmth, with caretaking, with reassurance that of course I'd be back, that I'd stay in touch, that I'd keep helping however I could. But I didn't do that this time.

I didn't ghost. I didn't slam a door. I just didn't reopen it. And that was new. There's a difference between slamming a door and simply closing it. One is about making a point. The other is about making peace.

I used to think closure had to be loud—that endings needed explanation, ceremony, or a final word to be real. But I've learned that some of the most powerful boundaries come without fanfare. They arrive quietly. In a pause. A decision. A deep breath followed by no reply.

And while I've learned to honor that truth personally, our institutions are still catching up. In so many professional and community settings, endings are expected to be packaged—explained, justified, tied with a bow. But maybe it's time we normalize quiet departures. The kind that honor both the role something played and the decision to move forward—without performance.

Not because the relationship didn't matter. Not because I wasn't hurt. But because I'm done bleeding energy into places that no longer feel aligned. This wasn't about bitterness. Or resentment. It was about reverence—for my healing, for my nervous system, and for the part of me that no longer needed to justify her exit just to feel at peace.

I didn't need to be seen as the "good one" on the way out. I just needed to be honest. And for me, that was the most radical act of transparency: choosing not to perform closure for someone else's comfort.

But some moments don't come with words at all. Sometimes, the dismissal isn't spoken—it's felt. A flicker of disbelief. A subtle eye roll. A shift in tone that says, *You're not capable. You're not serious. You're too much.*

I've spent my whole life decoding those looks. I know what they mean. And I used to let them get to me—used to collapse or overexplain or second-guess myself. But this time was different.

At the beginning of 2025, I entered an eating disorder recovery program. It was partial hospitalization—full days, six days a week. I wasn't staying overnight, but it consumed my schedule and nervous system. After thirty years of disordered eating, I finally admitted that therapy and medication weren't enough. I needed structure. I needed support. I needed to stop pretending food wasn't still in charge.

I chose the clinic carefully. I researched options, read reviews, weighed my possibilities. But something felt off almost immediately. On day three of the program, during my first meeting with the clinic's psychiatrist, she began suggesting that I might be bipolar—thirty minutes into our conversation. Another therapist later implied that my confidence in group was actually a manic episode. I'll talk more about that later—but what mattered in that moment was this: I was not in a healing environment. I was in a place that pathologized the very traits I had worked so hard to reclaim.

Still, I didn't flee impulsively. I made a plan to leave with integrity. Before walking away, I needed to prove to myself I could handle life outside the program—that I could follow a meal plan, nourish my body, and hold myself with structure and care. So I set up tests for myself. I tracked. I ate. I stayed present even when I didn't want to. And I did it. I proved to myself that I didn't need to stay in an environment that didn't respect me just to stay accountable to my healing. So I left.

Over the next few weeks, something shifted. The mental space that had once been consumed by survival slowly opened into possibility. Without daily appointments or emotional overdrive, I could think again—really think—about what I wanted next. And what emerged surprised even me.

I began planning a four-month spiritual journey through Southeast Asia. It wasn't a whim. It was a dream I'd carried quietly for years—one that always felt too big, too indulgent, too risky. But now, with distance from the clinic and proof that I could care for myself on my own terms, I finally felt ready. I was reclaiming something—not just my appetite, but my aliveness.

By the time I returned to the clinic a few weeks later for a routine nutrition check-in, the trip was fully mapped out. I had researched flights, planned volunteer placements, coordinated housing, and designed it as both an act of healing and a test of trust in myself. I was grounded. I was clear. And I was proud.

So when I sat across from the woman who ran the clinic and told her about my plans, I wasn't asking for approval. I was sharing something sacred—the first real glimpse of my next chapter. And she rolled her eyes. Not dramatically. Just enough to send a message.

It was subtle. But not soft. That single flick of disbelief carried the full weight of a lifetime of dismissal. It said, *You're being unrealistic. You're not ready. You're still sick. Who do you think you are?*

But this time, I didn't flinch. I didn't spiral. I didn't soften the truth or sell myself short. I just kept talking—calm, grounded, proud. Because I didn't need her belief to make it real. I had my own.

And in that moment, I doubled down. Not just on the trip, but on every dream I had ever tucked away to make other people more comfortable. I knew what it had cost me to live inside other people's limitations. And I was done paying.

But release doesn't always come with a dramatic ending. Sometimes, it arrives quietly—through the steady, sacred choice to loosen your grip on what you've outgrown. Because letting go isn't just about creating distance. It's about creating room for the future you can't yet see, for the version of you that hasn't fully arrived.

Because letting go isn't sterile. It's not a clean break or a quiet shelf-clearing. It's messy. Tender. Disorienting. Especially when the thing you're releasing once felt like purpose.

I've always had a hard time leaving things undone. I stayed in roles too long. Carried responsibilities I'd outgrown. Tried to resuscitate things that were already dying. Not because I didn't know how to move on, but because I didn't want to disappoint anyone. Because some part of me still believed that staying equaled loyalty. That letting go meant betrayal. But over the past year, that's started to shift.

During my time volunteering in Vietnam, I kept bumping into an old ache: the part of me that measured worth by how much I gave. I had shown up ready to serve—with money, time, effort, and enthusiasm. And when things got hard, when I saw harm I couldn't unsee, when I chose to speak up and step back—something deeper stirred. A quieter truth emerged. *You don't have to keep giving to prove your goodness.*

That truth haunted me. Because for most of my life, giving had been my currency. My camouflage. My justification for taking up space. But the version of me I'm becoming—she doesn't measure her value by her sacrifice.

So I let go. Not just of a role, or a relationship, or a donation pipeline. I let go of the identity that told me I had to be essential to be safe—that my worth was something I had to constantly earn through overgiving. And that's when *See Through* rose to the surface—not just as a book, but as a decision.

The idea for this book didn't begin in Vietnam. It had been bubbling for over a year. I'd even started writing it about six months before that trip, threading together stories and reflections that didn't quite belong anywhere else yet—but I knew they mattered. I always have multiple manuscripts in motion, catching different layers of my truth before they fully take shape.

At the time, I thought I'd publish something else first—a book for students, aligned with my new academic coaching business, *Prep 4 Higher Ed*. That book was nearly finished. It would have been the more "polished" move. The strategic one. And I still love that work. I still plan to release that book and support students in new ways.

But after what unfolded in Vietnam—the rupture, the reckoning, the boundary I held instead of explaining myself—I knew this had to come first. Because this book isn't about strategy. It's about survival. It's about soul.

It's not just for readers. It's for me. For the version of me who kept disappearing behind the expectations of others—the one who contorted herself into usefulness, helpfulness, and invisibility, just to belong.

That student-focused book would have taken me in a different direction. One I still want. But this book is what brought me home. And I had to write it before I could move forward—for me, and for everyone like me who's still trying to reclaim their place in their own life.

I'm tired of vanishing. And I don't want to go alone. Because this isn't just about telling my story; it's about making space for the stories so many of us were never allowed to voice. The ones we tucked away to stay palatable. The ones we polished to be accepted. The ones we never wrote because we didn't think anyone could hold them—including ourselves.

A version of me that had been camouflaged for most of my life finally stepped forward. She had always existed—I'd seen glimmers of her in moments of clarity, in flashes of rebellion, in the private pages of my journals. But this time, she wasn't hiding. And I was proud of her. Not because she was impressive, but because she was real—and no longer willing to perform her way into safety. She wasn't trying to earn her place anymore. She had arrived.

That shift didn't happen on a mountaintop. It happened in the aftermath of letting go. It happened when I stopped performing loyalty, stopped managing perception, stopped hemorrhaging energy to stay likable. It happened when I finally believed I didn't need to explain or justify my truth to honor it.

The space that opened wasn't just physical; it was energetic. Emotional. Creative. And I needed that space—to breathe, to heal, to write this. Because if I had stayed entangled, I don't think this book would have been born. At least not like this. Not with this kind of clarity. Not with *her*—the truest version of me—finally at the center of the page.

But stepping into truth doesn't mean you're done unraveling. It doesn't mean the doubts vanish or that your voice always comes out clean. Sometimes, the release is followed by a tremble—a wave of vulnerability you didn't see coming. Because once you stop hiding, people start to look. And once you start telling the truth, you can't always control how it's received.

I thought claiming my voice would feel like freedom. And it did. But it also came with whiplash—the ache of exposure, the fear of being misunderstood, the temptation to crawl back into the versions of me that kept things safer.

What no one tells you is that the moment after you speak—the silence, the echo, the wondering if you went too far. That's when the real work begins—not in the telling, but in the staying.

And here's what else I've learned—you're allowed to change. You're allowed to walk away from dynamics you once tolerated, even if they once felt like the safest place you knew. You don't owe anyone consistency when consistency comes at the cost of yourself.

Just because you said yes before doesn't mean you're not allowed to say no now. That's not betrayal. That's alignment. That's growth. Saying no is its own kind of release—the breath that finally reaches your ribs, the weight sliding off your shoulders. And if someone can't meet you in that evolution, that doesn't make your boundary wrong. It just means you've finally let go of needing their approval.

See Through Reflections

1. Personal Reflection

- Where in your life have you been praised for your generosity, patience, or resilience—even when it was costing you something vital?

- What relationships or dynamics have required you to shape-shift to stay connected?

- Where are you still cushioning your "no" to make it easier for someone else to hear?

2. Group or Cultural Exploration

- In your community, family, or workplace, how are boundaries typically received? Are they welcomed, ignored, resented, respected?

- How do you think gender, culture, or power dynamics have shaped your relationship to boundary-setting?

- What would it look like to normalize quiet exits—where no one has to perform closure to be seen as kind or respectful?

3. Somatic/Embodied Practice

- Recall a recent moment when you felt your "no" but didn't speak it—or spoke it and then overexplained. Where did that hesitation live in your body?

- Place your hand gently on that part of your body. Say softly, "I don't owe anyone a performance to be at peace." Let the words land. Let your body soften. Let your truth be enough.

CHAPTER 4
The Transparency Hangover

When I decided *See Through* was meant to be next, I poured myself into it. I worked for hours each day—adding scenes, rewriting sections, chasing threads I hadn't expected to find. At night, I'd lie in bed still buzzing—a sentence, a memory, a new truth tugging at me until I reached for my phone to capture it. I couldn't stop thinking about how to make it all fit.

And for a while, I questioned it. Was this healthy? Was I slipping back into old survival patterns—the overworking, the obsession, the drive to prove? Or was something else happening? What I've come to realize is this: not every intensity is a trauma response. Some intensities are devotion.

I've always had the capacity to go all in—to pour myself into a vision so fully that the outside world disappears. That kind of focus isn't typical. And it's rarely praised. For most of my life, it's been misunderstood. Pathologized. I was called obsessed, compulsive, or some other form of *too much*. I was told that something must be wrong with me.

And maybe sometimes, there was. Maybe, in the past, I used intensity to outrun grief. To numb pain. To prove I deserved to exist. But this time is different.

This isn't escape; it's a homecoming. I'm not dissociating; I'm present. I'm moved to tears by what I'm creating, connected to my body, feeding myself, choosing this. Not because I need to prove anything, but because—for the first time—I know what it feels like to build from clarity instead of fear.

The truth is, I'm working more than most people would consider "balanced." But I'm not trying to be most people. I'm writing the book of my life—the book that could change other people's lives—and I am fully immersed in it. This isn't avoidance. This is alignment.

And yes, there's a voice in my head—the old voice—that asks if I'm doing too much. That wonders if I've crossed the line from purpose into pathology. But then I remember something I said out loud in a conversation with ChatGPT—and something ChatGPT said back to me:

"If you were a man with this kind of intensity and vision, many people would call you 'disciplined,' 'driven,' or 'elite.' But because you're a woman—and a woman healing from trauma—your ambition is often misinterpreted as a disorder."

That hit me hard because it was familiar. I'd wrestled with that thought for years, and hearing it reflected back in plain language landed like a mirror, not a mandate. I've been labeled for most of my life. But I'm no longer willing to carry those labels as mine. I'm not broken for working hard. I'm not disordered for dreaming big. I'm not dangerous for being devoted.

Yes, I am intense. Yes, I go all in. And no, I don't want to be rescued from that. Because when my focus is in service of my truth— not my survival—it's not obsession. It's freedom. But even freedom has its echoes; especially in a world that doesn't always know what to do with women like me.

People have told me my whole life to slow down. That I was doing too much. And maybe sometimes I was, but not always for the reasons they claimed. Sometimes it wasn't about care at all. It was about projection. About their own unease. About how my pace forced them to see the goals they weren't chasing, the risks they weren't taking, the parts of themselves they had silenced for years.

And sometimes, it wasn't even that deep. They just didn't want me to shine that brightly. Didn't want me to make them look bad. So they dressed it up as concern. But underneath the "just worried about you" was often resentment, envy, or fear.

Still, I kept going. Because when I get enthralled in something, I can sit for hours. Time bends. Focus sharpens. The rest of the world fades. But with the degeneration in my spine—and the way I clench my jaw or tighten my back muscles without realizing—there are moments when my mind wants to keep writing, but my body is screaming for me to move. And I feel conflicted. Which part of me do I listen to?

These days, I start by checking in. How long have I been sitting? Am I pushing through something stressful, like writing a story that's hard to recall? Could a stretch help, or am I just trying to avoid the discomfort of the memory? If I'm close to finishing a thought, I jot a quick note, mark where I left off, and then get up. And when I notice myself gripping, I unclench my jaw, roll my shoulders, and let my breath drop lower—small releases that remind my body it doesn't have to earn this page.

That's a win for me. A big one. Because after years of overriding my body—through disordered eating, through sex I didn't want, through mountain climbs with a heavy pack on a degenerating spine—choosing to pause and listen is no small thing. It's sacred.

So sometimes I stretch. Sometimes I dance to a song I love. Sometimes I watch ten minutes of *The Golden Girls* and let myself laugh. Because that, too, is healing. That, too, is devotion.

And still, there were afternoons when the blur crept in—fan whirring, heat pressing at my back, the edge of the desk against my forearms. Even with all the tools I've gathered—from yoga, from healing, from learning how to stay with myself—there were days in Vietnam, curled over my laptop, when I questioned whether I was doing it wrong.

Because that internalized doubt doesn't live in a vacuum; it's echoed and reinforced by the systems we live in. Workplaces, leadership pipelines, and even healing communities still confuse composure with credibility. When women show up fully resourced and unapologetically focused, we're often met with suspicion. But when men do it, we call it leadership. The labels may be personal, but the pattern is systemic.

And when you've spent your life being measured against those distorted metrics—praised for being palatable, punished for being powerful—it's easy to lose track of what your own truth even feels like. That's when survival strategies start to look like identity. That's when the chase begins.

I used to chase mountains to feel free. To prove I was more than the girl who'd been hurt. More than the body that had once been controlled. Summits became symbols. Each one a way to say, "I'm strong. I'm whole. I made it."

But somewhere along the way, I learned that healing isn't always found at the top. Sometimes it's in the softening. The pause. The moment you stop pushing long enough to ask: Do I actually want to go further—or have I already arrived?

That's been one of the hardest lessons to carry into my writing life. The idea that devotion doesn't have to mean depletion. That being all-in doesn't require me to be wrung out. The mountains taught me that. That control is not the same as safety. That surrender isn't weakness; it's trust.

And when I find myself reaching for another line, another paragraph, another scene—I pause and ask: Am I building something sacred? Or just trying to outrun the silence? That pause is the same crossroads I've met in classrooms, on trails, and in rooms that tested my boundaries: keep performing, or release the role and feel what follows. Again and again, I've had to choose which voice to honor— my own, or the ones that told me massive action was the only path to greatness. Sometimes those voices lit a fire in me. But other times, they scorched me.

And when that happened, when the pressure to be impressive collided with the old voice of Diablo—my inner critic—whispering I was too much, not enough, or doing it wrong, I needed something to come between them. I needed a voice that belonged to *me*.

I had released so much; the roles, the masks, the habits of explaining. But release isn't always relief. Sometimes it leaves an ache. A space. A silence. And I was sitting in it. I didn't want to rush to fill it with someone else's approval, or the noise of productivity, or the pressure to prove I was doing it "right."

I was sitting in the space it left. I needed something stronger than other people's rules to anchor me. So I gave that something to myself; I wrote the upcoming manifesto. Not to share; not at first. But to survive the moments when shrinking felt safer than standing tall.

I used to think the trail was the only place where I could feel this level of clarity—where every step was stripped of pretense, where the only thing I had to prove was that I could keep going. But writing *See Through* has shown me another kind of pilgrimage. One where the terrain is emotional, not physical. Where the risks are quieter but just as real. And where rest—not just movement—is part of the journey.

Looking back, I realize that was my *transparency hangover*— that space between release and relief. The quiet grief that follows true letting go, when the performance finally drops and the weight you've carried shows itself. The shame after the truth. The doubt that echoes after clarity.

Before I ever dared to write this book, I had to learn how to sit with what it would require of me—and also how to recognize when I was slipping back into old patterns. That's been the work: not perfection, but presence. Not avoiding the intensity, but discerning whether it's aligned. And that didn't come from ambition; it came from practice. Years of learning to stay. To breathe. To be with discomfort without letting it devour me. Because you can't walk into trauma without a fire-retardant suit.

And I wish more systems understood that. I've seen trauma-informed language co-opted without trauma-informed culture—in classrooms, hospitals, boardrooms. We teach people how to regulate individually, but rarely ask how group dynamics or institutional expectations dysregulate them in the first place.

That's what yoga and meditation gave me. Not a way to erase pain, but a way to hold it differently. A way to build internal scaffolding strong enough to revisit what once would have collapsed me. I don't think I could have written *See Through* five years ago. I didn't yet have the tools to feel what needed to be felt without getting lost in it.

Back then, pain meant panic. Stillness meant spiraling. But now I know: sitting with pain isn't a test of composure. It's a practice—not perfection—built on repetition. Grit. Self-trust. The ability to sit with a memory without reenacting it. The ability to feel something rise and not reach for a distraction, a diagnosis, or a justification.

I used to think transparency meant sharing everything—the whole timeline, the full flood of grief, the uncensored wound. But I've since learned that real transparency doesn't require reliving everything. It requires resourcing. It requires discernment. And it requires honoring your own threshold for intensity—not pushing through it just to prove how "real" you're willing to be.

Visibility doesn't always feel like empowerment. Sometimes, it feels like exposure. Like an echo chamber of old doubts and new projections. Like the very thing you worked so hard to reclaim—your voice—is suddenly on trial.

I had come so far, but my nervous system hadn't caught up yet. It still believed I needed to shrink to stay safe. So I gave myself something to hold onto.

My See Through Manifesto

(For the woman who refuses to shrink—even when the world tells her to)

I'm not broken for wanting more.
I'm not too much for loving hard, working deep, or dreaming big.
I'm not here to be palatable—
I'm here to be powerful.

I'm not a machine.
But I am relentless, devoted, and clear.
When my work aligns with my truth,
it becomes an act of healing—not harm.
My ambition is not a symptom of trauma—
it's what helped me survive it.

I don't owe stillness to those who've never carried this kind of fire.
I won't slow down for those who never dared to begin.
I know how to rest. I know how to rise.
And I trust myself to choose which one I need.

My highs don't make me unstable.
My lows don't make me unworthy.
They make me human.
A human who has survived more than most—and still chooses to
feel.

The story I'm writing is not just a book—
It is a lighthouse. A legacy. A revolution on the page.

I refuse to abandon it—or myself—
for the comfort of people
who mistake sensitivity for weakness,
and resilience for disorder.

Let them call it obsession.
I call it devotion.

I am See Through—
not because I'm exposed,
but because I'm no longer contorting.

Transparency without resourcing is self-destruction in disguise, a release with no net. It's one thing to open the door to your pain; it's another to build the capacity to walk through it without collapsing. That's why I don't subscribe to *performative suffering* anymore—the belief that pain only matters if it's visible. I've lived that script. I've watched people bleed emotionally just to prove they're being honest. And I'm done with that. But being done with it doesn't mean I never revisit it. Shame still finds its way in, especially when I'm on the edge of something big.

While I was in Ho Chi Minh City, spending long hours writing *See Through*, I was also reviewing the audiobook recordings for *Moving Forward*— a book I had published two years earlier. One afternoon, as I listened back for errors so they could be fixed before I left the city, I felt that familiar voice returning. My mind was already focused on finding mistakes—and it went into overdrive. The criticism. The doubt. Diablo, loud and alive. I hated how different my voice sounded from chapter to chapter. I hated how critical I became of the tone, the pace, even the pause between lines. What should've been a celebration of how far I'd come quickly turned into a spiral. Or at least, it *wanted* to.

Part of the shame wasn't just about the sound of my voice—it was about how much better *See Through* already felt. The writing was clearer. The insight deeper. And instead of feeling proud, I felt exposed. What if people don't believe I wrote this? What if it's *too* good? What if I shine so brightly that people try to tear it down?

That day, it wasn't just the audiobook that cracked something open—it was the reality that I had just reached out to formally resign from my last job. I hadn't taught in over two months, but I was still technically listed as an adjunct. That job had been one of my last safety nets—financially, structurally, even psychologically. Letting it go made everything feel real. And raw. And irreversible. I wanted to run. To downplay what I was building. To shrink.

But instead, I did something new. I reread my manifesto—slowly, out loud, line by line. Not as a declaration, but as a lifeline. And then I told the truth of what I was feeling. I didn't push it away or reframe it; I let it exist. I wrote it down. I let myself be scared and keep going. I didn't disappear into productivity or punishment, didn't spiral. I paused. I stayed. And that—more than any paragraph I finished or page I edited—was the real win.

Because sometimes, growth doesn't look like power. It looks like reading your own words back to yourself, whispering them like prayer, and refusing to abandon your truth—even when fear begs you to.

Staying present takes practice. Not just in moments of clarity, but in the messy, middle moments—the ones where your instinct is to explain, to flee, to brace. That's where I've had to return to what my body already knows.

Stillness isn't surrender. It's strategy. The same way I learned to steady my breathing through discomfort on the mat, I've learned to meet discomfort on the page. To let the truth come, without needing to overexplain it. To let myself pause before reacting. To ground instead of spiral. That's what yoga taught me: presence over panic. Consciousness over collapse.

Writing this book hasn't been about extracting every ounce of pain—it's been about being honest with what I'm ready to carry. And trusting that what I don't say yet will still be there when I am.

That kind of discernment—of what to hold, what to release, and when—isn't just something I do on the page. It follows me into daily life. Into decisions that may seem small, but carry deeper weight.

I signed up for the Cu Chi tunnels tour partly because I needed to get out of the city. I've never been a city person—I'm a country girl at heart—and after weeks in Ho Chi Minh City, I wanted to end my time in Vietnam with something that brought me closer to nature. The tour was paired with a visit to the Mekong Delta, and it felt like the right blend of movement, history, and open space.

I knew the Cu Chi tunnels carried deep historical weight. And I also knew that shooting an AK-47 would be one of the optional activities. I had gone back and forth about it for days—unsure of what I'd choose. I didn't make my final decision until we were nearly at the firing range.

Part of me was curious. I had grown up learning how to shoot and used to be a good shot. I wondered what it would feel like to hold a weapon so powerful. I thought about the young soldiers—some barely teenagers—forced to make life-or-death decisions over and over again, staring down the barrel of guns they may not have even wanted to hold.

But another part of me felt uneasy. Would it seem like I was glamorizing war? Disrespecting the weight of what had happened there?

I shared my dilemma with the tour guide. I told him I was conflicted. That I was American, and a part of me didn't feel right about it. He told me plainly: placing a gun range on an old battlefield "is not a really nice idea." His tone was respectful, but firm. And though I had already been leaning toward not participating, his honesty helped me listen more closely to what my body already knew. My heart was telling me it wasn't right. So I didn't.

Even just approaching the gun range was jarring. The sound of multiple guns going off at once was deafening. It made me think about how terrifying it must have been for soldiers on both sides. No peace. No quiet. Just the relentless roar of fear and fire.

Later, as we walked together, the guide pointed out one of the original air vents used during the war—small, discreet, nearly hidden. He told me the larger ones we'd seen earlier were replicas made for tourists. There was pressure, he explained. Tour guides compete to keep their groups happy. They need to keep people moving so everyone can take their pictures. To avoid conflict and accommodate large crowds, they built multiple tunnels and vents to replicate the experience.

I understood the business side of it; I really did. These attractions draw tourists. They create jobs. They generate tax revenue. And still... it made me ache. Something about it felt like history was being commodified. Like pain was being packaged. That ache wasn't just about tourism; it was the grief of recognizing a pattern I knew in myself—times I'd packaged pain before I was ready, just to survive. I thought of the workers—the people doing the labor to maintain these sites—and how little of that money likely makes it into their hands.

And then I thought of myself. How many times had I worried that I was prostituting my story? That I was allowing the voyeuristic public to peer into the most wounded parts of my past and present? That's what it felt like, sometimes—especially early in my business. But I kept going. Because I've seen the impact. I've seen what happens when people feel less alone. Less ashamed. I've seen what happens in me.

Every time I tell my story, the pain gets a little less sharp. And when the painful parts stop screaming so loud, it becomes easier to hear the joyful ones. It becomes easier to welcome new experiences; even complicated ones like this. I'm sure it's the same for countries. For cultures. For communities trying to reclaim their narrative.

There are some who criticize the War Remnants Museum in Vietnam for being too one-sided. For not telling "all sides" of the story. But maybe that's the point. Maybe it's Vietnam's way of telling their story—through their own eyes. Maybe there's power in that. Healing, even. Because being able to say, "This is what happened to us," is a form of freedom.

I asked the tour guide if giving these tours was difficult for him. He nodded. "It used to be very hard," he said. "But over time, it gets easier." Maybe it's like that for all of us—the more we tell the truth, the less it crushes us. Not because the truth gets lighter, but because we get stronger. More honest. More equipped to hold it.

Before I ever wrote a word of *See Through*— before I ever said anything out loud in the eating disorder recovery program—I recorded a voice memo. Past midnight, with the apartment silent around me, the glow of my phone felt like the only witness I could bear. I was spiraling, and I knew I needed help. I knew treatment was coming. But I also knew that if I didn't name the hardest truths now, I might walk into that program still pretending.

So I opened the voice memo app and just spoke. I didn't filter or posture. I wasn't trying to write a story or craft a breakthrough. I was just trying to get honest with myself. I said things like:

"I use gossip to feel important."
"I chase visibility because I don't know how to feel valuable without it."
"I'm scared that if I stop proving myself, I'll disappear."
"I'm not addicted to drama—I'm addicted to feeling like I matter."

I said those things not because anyone asked, but because I needed to hear myself say them. I needed to stop hiding behind awareness and own the behavior. Not just the wound underneath it, but the impact it was having. The pain I was carrying—and the pain I was passing along.

It wasn't graceful. It wasn't eloquent. But it was real. And it felt like stepping into a different kind of integrity—the kind that doesn't depend on applause. The kind that's willing to drop the act to reclaim the person underneath it.

That recording became my baseline. My map. My way of saying, *If I get lost in this process, bring me back here.* Bring me back to this voice—the one that's not trying to be liked, just trying to be free. And I did get lost. More than once. But I kept returning to that voice. To that truth. Because even when it's messy, even when it hurts, naming what's real is what keeps me steady.

Still, clarity doesn't erase reflex. Healing doesn't cancel out history. I wish I could say that awareness always translates into action. But healing isn't linear—and even with all the tools, all the insight, there are still moments when I react in ways I don't recognize, or regret the second they happen.

One afternoon in Vietnam, while teaching an English class, a boy swore at another student. I'd calmly explained then that we wouldn't be using those English words in the classroom. In the next class, he swore again. This time, he was sitting right next to me. And before I had time to think, I lightly slapped his hand. Not hard—only the tips of my fingers made contact. But it surprised both of us. And it gutted me.

I'd never done that before. I didn't even know where it came from. Except I did. I'd seen it modeled at that very school. I'd watched other staff members do the same thing—a light slap to a student's hand when they were acting out. I didn't like it, but I tried to rationalize it. They're doing the best they can, I told myself. They're overwhelmed. They don't have the training or the support they need.

But then I did it. Was it stress? The long days? The relentless humidity? The lack of air conditioning? I don't know. What I do know is that the shame arrived instantly. A sharp wave of disbelief and guilt that hit me in the gut and hasn't fully left since.

I wanted to disappear. And I wanted to judge myself. How could I have been so critical during the clips incident when I had my own moment like this? How dare I hold anyone else accountable when I couldn't even stop myself?

But I also remembered something important: I didn't think the staff member who used the clips deserved punishment—I thought she deserved support. So maybe I didn't deserve punishment either.

Even though the shame was strong, I didn't want it to silence me. So before the next class, I pulled the student aside. I told him I was sorry for slapping his hand. I said it wasn't right—no matter how small or reflexive it seemed. He shrugged. "It's okay," he said. "I've had teachers do way worse." I told him that wasn't okay either. And then we moved on. The other students came in, and we continued class. But the moment never left me.

On my last day, I asked him to stay behind again. I told him I really enjoyed having him in class. He looked confused and asked why. I told him he was smart. And funny. And that those two things don't always go together, but he had both.

He made a comment about being stupid and fat—something I'd heard him say before, often with sarcasm, sometimes with bite. So I told him the truth. That I had been overweight at his age, too. That people weren't always kind to me, either. That I heard him say mean things about himself—and I used to do that, too.

I told him people said terrible things about me when I was growing up. But they were wrong about me—and they're wrong about him, too. He nodded, quietly. Said he knew I was right. Said he should ignore them.

I told him it wouldn't be easy. That the more potential people see in you, the more they'll try to tear you down. That being smart and different can make you a target. But that he was going to be okay. I told him he was special. That I believed in him.

That exchange—quiet, imperfect, human—didn't undo what came before. But it softened something. And with that softening came an ache; the grief of noticing how quickly I still reach for control when fear rises. It wasn't erasure, but it was a small, honest repair. A *transparent repair*. One rooted in ownership, not show—in humility, not theatrics. It didn't excuse what happened. But it interrupted the pattern, and that matters.

It reminded me that even in the moments we wish we could take back, there's still a chance to show up differently next time. To tell the truth. To stay human. To keep choosing love, even when it breaks our own heart open.

I wish more schools, workplaces, and community spaces made room for that kind of repair—the small, real, unpolished moments that don't erase harm, but interrupt its repetition. Too often, we're taught that if harm wasn't catastrophic, it doesn't count. But silence after harm reinforces shame—and collective repair starts by normalizing truth without theatrics.

Looking back, I can see that the moment with that student didn't come out of the blue. It wasn't just the heat or the long days or the cultural modeling I'd witnessed. It rose from somewhere older— somewhere deeper. It rose from a nervous system shaped by childhood roles I was never meant to hold.

I'm the oldest of three. By the time I was nine, my parents had divorced, and I had already stepped into the role of second adult. I helped care for my younger sisters. I supported my mom emotionally. I stayed strong, even when I didn't feel strong, because I had to. That same year, I also began being sexually abused. Which meant I wasn't just adultified emotionally—I was stripped of the right to be a child at all.

So I learned early that being lovable meant being helpful. That staying safe meant staying in control. That order wasn't optional; it was survival.

Those lessons don't just disappear with age or therapy. They live in the body. And sometimes, they resurface in moments we least expect—like when a student swears in a classroom I'm trying to hold together, and something inside me panics. Reacts. Reaches for order. Not because I want to harm, but because some old, unspoken part of me believes it's my job to fix it. That if I don't stop it now, something worse might happen. That I'm the one who must keep everyone safe.

I see that pattern now. The way early adultification wires you to become a savior, a fixer, a protector—not out of ego, but out of fear. Out of necessity. Because when your own safety once depended on your ability to hold it all together, your body remembers what to do— even if your mind has long since moved on.

This isn't an excuse. It's a reckoning. Because this is what trauma reenactment can look like: not just self-destruction, but control. Not just collapse, but overcorrection. And if we don't name those patterns—if we don't trace the behavior back to its roots—we end up recycling shame instead of transforming it.

I'm not proud of what I did. But I am proud that I didn't run from it. That I owned it. That I apologized. That I let myself feel the shame—not to punish myself, but to stay present with the version of me who still, after everything, sometimes forgets that safety doesn't have to be earned through control.

Because that's what I want people to understand: this kind of slip doesn't make you a monster. It makes you human. A human who was once overburdened, over-responsibilized, and forced to grow up too fast. And the more we talk about that—honestly, without defensiveness—the less power those unconscious reflexes have over us. The more we reclaim the right to pause. To repair. To write a different ending.

And maybe even more importantly—the more we push back on the myth of the "ideal survivor." The one who never slips. The one who always knows better. The one who heals in a straight line and never repeats old patterns. That ideal doesn't help us; it haunts us. It shames us into silence. It makes us hide the very moments that most need care.

There are so many reasons my perfectionism began—and just as many reasons it's lingered, even inside my healing. Sometimes it tells me I'm not allowed to regress after making progress. That once I know better, I must always do better. But that's not healing; that's a show. And I don't want to perform recovery. I want to live it.

And living it means making room for imperfection. For repair. For the pauses and the pivots. For the truth that healing isn't linear, and that growth doesn't always look like progress. Because here's what

I didn't see at first: not all trauma looks like collapse. Sometimes it looks like achievement. Sometimes it hides inside the very things people praise you for.

I used to think trauma only looked like flashbacks—like panic attacks, shaking hands, or spiraling thoughts. And yes, sometimes it does. I've lived those moments. I still do. But over time, I've learned that trauma doesn't always announce itself loudly. Sometimes, it shows up in disguise—in the quiet ways we learn to survive without being seen.

It can sound like "I'm fine," said so often you almost believe it. It can feel like exhaustion that no amount of rest touches. It can look like relentless overfunctioning: staying late, saying yes, smiling wide, trying to make everything okay—not out of joy, but out of fear. Fear that if you stop performing, you'll be seen as difficult. Or worse, as unworthy.

Sometimes trauma doesn't erupt. It manages. It perfects. It performs. It micromanages other people's perceptions so you don't spiral into shame. It convinces you that control is safety, and visibility is a threat—unless you're useful, composed, and easy to digest.

And it blends in. Especially in high-performance environments where overfunctioning gets mistaken for drive. I've watched entire teams celebrate someone's hustle while missing the burnout beneath it. When trauma wears a blazer and speaks in bullet points, no one thinks to call it pain.

For a long time, I didn't realize I was suppressing trauma. I thought I was being strong. I thought staying busy and showing up meant I was okay. But I wasn't. I was bypassing grief I hadn't named. Carrying pain I hadn't acknowledged. And when pain has nowhere to go, it finds its own exit—through shutdown, through burnout, through symptoms without clear names.

There's a thin, often invisible line between strength and suppression—and I've crossed it more than once. Not because I was lying, but because I'd spent my life surviving by staying composed. I was praised for being insightful, grounded, and wise. But I knew how to say the right thing long before I knew how to feel the real thing. The scariest part wasn't the pain itself—it was how easy it became to hide it, even from myself.

That's part of what makes high-functioning trauma so insidious—it performs wellness while hiding the wreckage. It convinces people you couldn't possibly be that hurt, because you're still so helpful. So articulate. So put together.

There were years when I was teaching trauma recovery while quietly unraveling inside my own body. I had the language. I had the curriculum. I could quote van der Kolk, cite Maté, explain the polyvagal theory. I knew how trauma lived in the nervous system—I even taught others how to regulate theirs. But I hadn't let it touch me. Not really. Because touching it would've required me to let go of the illusion of safety. And I wasn't ready for that yet.

That's the thing about being "the expert"—people listen. They nod. They tell you how clear, how insightful, how articulate you are. And you start to believe that knowing is healing. That being able to name something means you've worked through it. But that's not how the body works. You can't out-teach your own nervous system. You can't out-talk your own grief. And mine was tired of being ignored.

I would stand in front of rooms or Zoom squares, walking people through grounding exercises and the stages of trauma response. But inside, I was still frozen. Still fleeing. Still bracing. I spoke with conviction. But I didn't feel safe. I wasn't grounded. I was surviving.

After that moment in the classroom in Vietnam—after I faced the part of me that didn't pause before reacting—I started to see it all more clearly. Not just the immediate shame, but the deeper thread. The one that had been running through everything for decades.

I've always been "the strong one." The composed one. The one who could explain what no one else could name. In so many spaces—healing spaces especially—I became "the wise one" way too early. I had metaphors. I had insight that sounded profound—and often was. But I didn't always have regulation. I didn't have a lived experience of safety. I had trauma and talent braided so tightly that I couldn't tell where one ended and the other began.

I could name my patterns, soothe a room, hold space for someone else's unraveling, but not always my own. In survival, usefulness became my currency. If I couldn't be safe, I'd be helpful. If I couldn't be loved without condition, I'd earn it through insight. If I couldn't feel it, I'd teach it.

Eventually, wisdom became a costume. One that protected me from judgment, but also from myself. I wore that costume for decades. Not out of manipulation, but out of muscle memory. It was how I stayed liked. How I stayed needed. How I stayed upright.

There's a fine line between sharing and self-abandonment, and I've crossed it more than once, even with good intentions. Because when truth-telling becomes a strategy to be palatable or praised, it stops being intimacy and starts becoming erosion. But erosion doesn't always happen in public. Sometimes, it happens quietly—when you let your guard down around someone you once believed was safe.

Not every betrayal is immediate. Some unravel slowly—subtle at first, then suddenly unmistakable.

Years ago, in my late thirties, I reconnected with one of my former high school teachers. He was older, composed, well-liked. I had trusted him.

It wasn't that we were especially close, but it was a small school—fewer than four hundred students across all grades—and our class had fewer than twenty. It was easy to talk with teachers, and he was one of the few men in my life back then who didn't make me feel unsafe. When I thought about the adults who had witnessed my teenage years, he stood out as someone who seemed respectful. Someone I believed saw me as a student, not a problem. Not a threat. Not a body.

We started chatting over social media—casual at first. Light catching up. A few exchanges about where we lived, what we'd been up to, and the possibility of meeting for dinner sometime between our cities. It felt innocent. Familiar. And I assumed that's all it was—a chance to connect, reminisce, maybe reflect on how far I'd come since high school.

Then, suddenly, he suggested we meet at "the hotel" first. Not *a* hotel. *The* hotel. Like it had already been discussed. Like it was obvious. Like this wasn't dinner—this was a different kind of arrangement entirely. I froze.

We had never spoken about a hotel. I implied nothing beyond dinner. There had never been anything romantic between us—not in high school, not after. And now, out of nowhere, this man who had once been in a position of authority over me was suggesting a private hotel meetup, as if it had been mutually understood all along. It wasn't just presumptuous. It was retraumatizing.

Because my teenage years were soaked in sexual trauma. And for so long, I didn't know who was safe. I didn't even know how to ask that question. Back then, I worked hard to be seen as the good one. The smart one. The safe one. And when a teacher treated me with respect, it felt like a small kind of relief. Like maybe I wasn't just a body to be used. Like maybe I could trust someone.

But now, decades later, I had to ask: Had he always seen me that way? Had he—even then—viewed me as a sexual object? Had I misread his kindness in the same way I'd misread so many others?

That message unraveled something I didn't even realize was still knotted. It made me doubt my memory. My discernment. My capacity to tell the difference between safety and performance. Because when someone you once trusted uses their silence as camouflage—and waits until you've relaxed your guard to reveal who they really are—it makes you question everything. Not just their intentions, but your own instincts.

I reread our messages over and over. Scanned every line I sent. Wondered if I had somehow given the wrong impression. Tried to figure out what I could have done differently. That spiral—that instinct to blame myself for someone else's violation—didn't come from nowhere. It came from a lifetime of trying to be safe in rooms that weren't.

And sometimes, the rooms weren't even rooms. They were trails. Friendships. Familiar places where I let my guard down—and still got hurt.

Years ago, I had a hiking partner I deeply trusted. We were never romantic. Never flirty. We'd spent countless hours on trails together, swapping stories, sharing snacks, hugging goodbye at trailheads—and not once had anything ever felt unsafe. I let my nervous system rest around him. He was significantly older, thoughtful, grounded. He felt… safe.

By the time this happened, I wasn't hiking as much. But we still stayed in touch. One night, we met for dinner in New York City—not something we'd done before, but it didn't feel unusual. We used to live farther apart, but after I moved to the city, we were closer. We'd spent so many hours together in the past—on trails, in conversation—that catching up over a meal just felt like an extension of that same rhythm. The terrain was different, but the connection felt familiar.

After dinner, he offered to drive me home. That wasn't strange either. We weren't on a mountain, but we were catching up like we would have been if we were. I wasn't scanning for threats. I wasn't guarded. I was just present.

When we got to my apartment, we stood on the sidewalk to say goodbye. And during what should have been a normal moment—a quick hug between old friends—he grabbed my ass with both hands, pulled me into him, and thrust his pelvis against me while looking up at the sky and groaning, "Ahh." My whole body froze.

I remember walking up to my apartment in shock, trying to convince myself that maybe it wasn't what it felt like. That maybe I was misreading. That surely someone who had always been respectful wouldn't just do that. But I wasn't misreading. My body knew.

What hit me hardest wasn't just the violation; it was the betrayal of safety. He hadn't just crossed a line. He'd waited until I had put down my guard—until I stopped practicing vigilance—and then showed me that safety had been an illusion. That moment didn't just trigger old trauma. It layered on new grief. For days after, I felt it in my body—the tight chest, the restless sleep, the bracing for a hand that wasn't there. I'll explore more of how that lingered in Chapter 6, but here's what mattered most in the moment: when you've spent years scanning for danger, finally feeling safe is its own kind of sacred. And having that safety ripped out from under you—by someone you trusted—teaches your body that even peace can be a setup.

Afterward, I kept replaying it. Not just the act itself, but the quiet before it. The comfort. The ease. The absence of armor. I wasn't performing that day. I wasn't narrating. I wasn't trying to impress or teach. I was just being, and it still cost me something.

And that cost haunted me—not just in that moment, but in the ones that followed. Because even when I wasn't being violated, I was still managing how I was perceived. People told me I was inspiring. And for a long time, I needed to hear that. It gave meaning to the mess. It made the story feel lighter. But there's a cost to being "the strong one"—to being the person who always has a takeaway, a quote, a next step. Eventually, it stopped being empowering and started becoming a role I didn't know how to step out of.

Even in private grief, I'd find myself narrating my pain. Turning moments into metaphors. Trying to find the lesson while I was still bleeding. It wasn't just emotional exhaustion—it was something deeper. A kind of visibility fatigue. Not the kind that comes from being watched, but the kind that comes from needing everything you feel to be useful. Like every ache must become a teachable moment. Like even your suffering must earn its place.

I used to call it spiraling whenever I felt the edge of a memory. The chest tightening. The old ache in my spine. The urge to flee. Those sensations used to signal the beginning of a breakdown—the first step on a staircase I always fell down. But I see it differently now. I'm not tumbling. I'm not lost. I'm just standing at the top of the spiral staircase I used to plummet down. And that awareness—that pause, that breath—is proof I'm not where I was. This isn't spiraling. This is body memory. This is emotional echo. This is trauma imprint, not dysfunction.

I used to think I had to erase the staircase entirely to be okay. But now I know: I don't need to destroy it. I just need to trust that I can stand on it without falling. That I can hold what's rising without being consumed. That I can feel deeply without disappearing. But holding it doesn't mean others see it. And that's what hurt the most.

There were times people would look to me for answers, and I'd give them. But later, I'd go home and cry. Not because I said too much. But because they saw the wise one. The wordsmith. The helper. Not the child who was still aching underneath it all.

I've since learned that insight doesn't equal integration. Just because I can explain something doesn't mean I've healed it. Some of my most honest moments haven't come when I had the right words, but when I finally stopped staging them. When I let myself cry instead of narrate. When I stopped being the group's mirror and became my own.

That's been especially hard to navigate while building a life coaching practice where I am the brand. Where people follow not just my work, but my life. It makes me question: What's for me? What's for them? What happens when those lines start to blur?

I catch myself taking pictures I don't need—not because I want to preserve the moment, but because I think I should document it. Before all of this, I never used to take pictures. I hiked hundreds of mountains, traveled across the country and the world, without ever texting a photo to anyone. I didn't post them. I didn't even save them. My default was solitude.

And in some ways, it still is. Even though I have a big personality—bubbly, animated, expressive—I feel most at ease when I'm by myself. That's when I don't have to think about who I'm trying to impress. When I don't have to wonder who I need to be to keep the energy up or make someone else feel comfortable.

Sometimes I wonder if my big personality is real—or if it's just a survival script I haven't fully unlearned. Because when I'm with people I love, I love to laugh. I love to bring joy. But it's also exhausting. Not because I'm pretending, but because I'm always managing. Always scanning. Always shaping myself in small ways to be what's needed.

And I'm tired of needing to be needed. I'm tired of mistaking appearances for connection. And I'm ready—not just to be seen—but to be felt. By myself, first. That clarity didn't come from pushing; it came from pausing. From choosing to listen instead of prove. And I know I'm not the only one navigating that blur between authenticity and optics.

It's not just about how we hold our own boundaries; it's about the kinds of boundaries our culture makes space for. In leadership circles, transparency is often praised in theory but punished in practice. We ask for authenticity but reward polish. Especially in fields built on personal narrative—therapy, coaching, teaching—we rarely name the toll of staying publicly open while privately unraveling.

And that act doesn't stay confined to our roles. It seeps into our relationships. Our intimacy. Our sense of self.

When I finally started listening, really listening, one truth that surfaced was this: my confusion around sex wasn't just about past partners—it was about past patterns. Patterns that taught me to use my body as currency. Patterns that blurred the line between affection and survival.

For a long time, I thought my sexuality was broken. I didn't have the words for it—not back then. But I knew something felt off. I'd sleep with people who didn't see me. I'd act like I wanted it, even when my body was numb. I'd confuse attention with intimacy, and urgency with desire. And afterward, I'd either spiral or disappear.

It wasn't about pleasure. It wasn't even about power. It was about pattern—a loop that said, *If I give enough of myself, maybe I'll finally feel real.*

I used to think that made me reckless. Irresponsible. Confused. But now I know: it made me human. A human shaped by trauma. A human whose earliest experiences of sex weren't about choice or connection—they were about survival.

The lines got blurry fast. Especially in my twenties. There were moments I wanted closeness, but not sex—and I couldn't tell the difference. Or I could, but I didn't think I was allowed to say no. Sometimes I'd crave the feeling of being wanted—until the second things started to escalate. Then I'd shut down. Go silent. Or go through the motions while silently wishing I could disappear. Sometimes, I'd want someone until they touched me. Other times, I'd want no one at all—and still say yes anyway.

I told myself I was empowered. That I was in control. But underneath the surface, I was acting out a script I didn't remember writing—one that equated visibility with value, and desire with danger. I didn't know how to feel safe in my body, so I made myself feel useful in someone else's.

It wasn't until years later that I learned the term *fawning*—the trauma response where people appease, over-accommodate, or abandon themselves to stay safe. That helped. But labels alone didn't free me. What helped most was learning to listen to my body and realizing that confusion doesn't mean dysfunction. It means something got crossed. Something got interrupted. Something got taken before I was ready to give.

Sometimes, when I talk about trauma and sexuality now, people ask me how I know the difference—between a trauma response and true desire. Between choosing sex and reenacting something old. And my answer is this: I don't always know. But I know what it feels like to override myself. And I've learned to stop doing that, even when it feels inconvenient. Even when it makes things awkward. Even when someone else doesn't understand.

That's what embodiment is for me now. Not constant certainty, but a commitment to checking in. To noticing. To naming what's real, even when I wish it wasn't.

And what's real is this: I've spent most of my life despising my body. There is so little I've looked at without flinching—especially during the weight gain required in eating disorder recovery. A few years ago, I had my eyebrows and lips tattooed and genuinely loved how I looked. It was one of the first times I felt at ease seeing my reflection. This time, in Ho Chi Minh City, I decided to get them touched up—along with a darker lip shade after testing a few lipsticks and realizing how much more I liked the way I looked with bolder color. I also added permanent eyeliner. I love how my blue eyes look with mascara, but I don't want to have to apply it every day.

These choices weren't about vanity—they were about ease. About reclaiming a sense of beauty that didn't feel like a battle every morning. Not beauty for approval, but beauty for peace. Acceptance and adjustment aren't opposites; both can honor a body that has carried a lot. In hot, humid climates where makeup melts and energy matters, these procedures simplify my life. They let me feel beautiful without needing a show. They make me feel like myself—not an edited version, but a supported one. This was release, too: comfort over correction, ease over endless self-fixing.

So when a woman who's known me since I was young and has generally been supportive over the years—messaged me privately to say I didn't need the tattooing, that I was already beautiful, it landed like a gut punch. I know she meant well. I know she thought she was offering kindness. But what it did was reopen an old wound. Because even when people tell me I'm beautiful, it doesn't override the degradation I've endured. It doesn't erase what my abuser said when I was twelve—that I was so disgusting, I should be grateful anyone even wanted to touch me. That's when the eating disorder started. That's when I began to disappear from myself. And some days, I'm still finding my way back.

When people think they have the right to weigh in on what I do with my body—especially something permanent—it infuriates me. Because what am I supposed to do with that feedback once it's done? It doesn't help. It only hurts. It layers on shame that didn't need to be there. And for what? To uphold some myth that self-acceptance means never wanting to change anything?

I've spent enough of my life trying to prove worthiness. These days, I'm learning how to claim comfort—not to hide who I am, but to feel at ease in who I've become. And that includes choosing what feels good in my body, without justification.

But feeling rooted in myself doesn't mean forgetting who I used to be. If anything, it means facing her more honestly than ever before.

Maybe that's why writing this book feels so raw. Because it's not just about healing from what happened. It's about reckoning with who I became in the aftermath—and choosing not to shame her, even when I no longer want to be her.

The mountains taught me how to listen for that truth. To trust that rest doesn't mean regression. That choosing ease over struggle is not a betrayal of strength; it's an evolution of it. And now, even off the trail, I carry those lessons with me. I don't need to summit something to feel alive. Sometimes, the bravest thing I can do is pause, exhale, and honor how far I've already come.

But honoring how far I've come also means reckoning with what I carried to get here—the truths I couldn't speak, the weight I didn't know I was holding, the grief that still echoes in the quiet moments. Not always loud, but always there. That's where we go next.

Grief is what surfaces when the script is finally set down; the ache that follows release. This is the hinge of the book: voice named its truth, cost tallied the price, and now grief loosens the grip so integration can choose what remains.

Chapter 5 isn't confession for confession's sake. It's integration in action—choosing what to share, how to hold it, and when to set it down. Because healing isn't about proving how much you've survived; it's about learning to live without abandoning yourself in the process.

See Through Reflections

1. Personal Reflection

- When have you told the truth and not felt immediate relief? What came up afterward—fear, shame, grief, doubt—and how did you meet yourself in that space?

- What's a moment you wish you could take back—not because you were malicious, but because you were unresourced or overwhelmed? What would self-forgiveness look like there?

- Have you ever confused being needed with being loved? How has that shaped your boundaries, your behavior, or your sense of worth—especially in relationships that prize your strength?

2. Group or Cultural Exploration

- In the communities you've been part of, what is praised more: vulnerability or composure? How does that shape what people feel safe to share?

- Have you ever watched someone reenact a trauma pattern—through control, overachievement, or perfectionism—and had it go unnoticed? How did others explain or respond to it?

- In your culture, what does "repair" usually look like—if it happens at all? What would a culture of transparent repair (honest, human, imperfect) require from its members?

3. Somatic/Embodied Practice

- Think of a moment when you slipped into an old role—the fixer, the performer, the strong one—even though you didn't want to. Where did your body tighten, brace, or go numb?

- Place your hands gently over that part of your body. Say softly, "I don't have to be perfect to be present. I don't have to collapse to be real." Let those words settle in, not to erase the pain but to anchor you in self-compassion.

Telling the Truth Without Telling It All

There's a quiet kind of courage in knowing what not to say. In choosing not to carry everything, even when you could. I used to think transparency meant exposure—that telling the truth required tearing yourself open. But grief has shown me otherwise. Grief loosens my grip; integration teaches my hands what to hold. Discernment is its own kind of truth-telling. Wholeness doesn't always look like revelation. Sometimes, it looks like restraint.

After finishing the audiobook for *Moving Forward*, I started pouring my whole self into *See Through*. I woke up with sentences already forming in my head. I moved through the day in a kind of trance; not foggy, but focused. Writing this book felt like stepping into a long-awaited conversation with my truest self. And for the first time, I didn't want to escape it. I wanted to be here—present, awake, all in.

But after days of near-constant flow, my back started whispering that I needed to move. So I did. I stepped away from my laptop, away from the words, and spent a few hours out in the city. I didn't go to relax. I went to do something I had been both avoiding and preparing myself for: visiting the War Remnants Museum in Ho Chi Minh City.

From everything I'd heard and read, I knew it would be graphic and upsetting. Still, I knew I needed to go. As much as I tend to avoid the news—the endless images of suffering, destruction, the ways humans ravage one another and the earth—I also know that bearing witness is part of my work. Not in a performative way. Not for shock or spectacle. But to let the truth move through me. To face the parts of the world I would rather not see, and let them mean something.

I didn't expect to be okay inside those walls. I wasn't. The photographs of torture. The disfigured bodies. The faces of children still affected by Agent Orange, decades after the war ended. It left me gutted. Not just for the Vietnamese people. Not just for the children. But for all of us. For everyone who's ever lived through war—and everyone who still will.

I grew up hearing about "the Vietnam War." But here, some spaces refer to it as *The American Vietnam War*. That shift in phrasing stopped me cold. I'd never heard it named that way before. It made me wonder how I was being perceived—walking through the museum as an American. But every conversation I've had since arriving in Vietnam has reminded me that most people here don't hold onto that war in bitterness. They hold it in memory. And they treat foreigners, even Americans, with kindness.

But memory can still be heavy. I walked through that museum overwhelmed by the weight of it—the brutality, the unnecessary cruelty, the kind of suffering that doesn't end when the last bullet is fired. It lingers in bodies, in bloodlines, in landscapes. Because war doesn't just belong to the pages of history books or the borders where it's fought. The names change. The landscapes shift. But the pattern—power sought through domination, ordinary people carrying extraordinary loss—repeats itself across centuries and continents. And it's still happening now, in places whose names will one day be etched into another museum wall.

And I thought about how every nation curates its stories—what's highlighted, what's hidden, and who gets to decide what counts as truth. The same thing happens closer to home, too: in families, in workplaces, in communities where someone decides the "official" version and the rest of us learn to live around it. These aren't just individual choices. They're collective ones. Cultural ones. And they shape how entire generations carry memory. I kept wondering: What do we do with a truth this big? How do we hold something we can't fix?

I'm someone who has always wanted to make things better. When I see injustice, I want to do something. But this—this was too big. There's no speech that undoes war. No outreach email that heals a wound this deep. So instead, I did the only thing I could: I let it hurt. I let myself feel helpless. I let the ache rise in my throat, and then I walked out and found a way to keep going.

That's what integration looks like, sometimes. Not fixing. Not numbing. Just staying long enough to let the truth move through you, but not consume you.

I needed to soothe my soul after that. And for me, that often comes through food—not as escape, but as comfort. As presence. As ritual. So I walked to a nearby restaurant called Hum Lounge—a vegetarian place I'd bookmarked days earlier but hadn't made time for yet.

Everything about it felt healing. The environment was peaceful. The menu explained the health benefits of each dish with care. The food came out like artwork—vibrant, intentional, offered with a smile. I sat down and let myself breathe. My jaw unhooked, my breath dropped lower, and the clench behind my eyes finally let go. And yet I was still so wound up that I knocked over my passion fruit drink, spilling it everywhere. I was mortified. It was a small mistake, but my body reacted like it was proof I didn't belong.

And the staff—they didn't scold, judge, or ignore me. They comforted me. Cleaned it up gently. Reassured me it was okay. And then, to my complete surprise, they brought me a fresh drink. The glass was cold in my hand; that first sip tasted like a yes to being cared for.

That moment broke me open in a different way. I had just walked through a museum filled with unspeakable horror—and now, I was being handed a small act of compassion that felt just as significant. Kindness, I'm learning, is not the opposite of pain. It's what makes pain survivable.

Later, I left a Google review for that restaurant. I needed to honor that moment. To let the world know that this place—this simple act of care—mattered.

There's a quote I once heard—from the French philosopher Simone Weil—that says, "Attention is the rarest and purest form of generosity." That day, the staff at Hum Lounge gave me that. They noticed. They responded. They reminded me I wasn't alone.

And it made me think about what happens when people *don't* respond. When we see something awful and walk away. When we keep quiet, not because we don't care, but because we don't know how to hold it—or because holding it would mean acknowledging how brutal the world can be. How unfair. How fragile.

I used to get angry at people for staying silent in the face of injustice. Sometimes, I still do. But I also understand it differently now. We all have bandwidth. We all have wounds. And some people, when they see pain, don't know how to move toward it without falling apart. They close their eyes—not because they're heartless, but because they're scared. Or tired. Or still healing themselves.

In movements, in families, in organizations—silence isn't always a sign of indifference. Sometimes it's a sign of collective fatigue. Of systems that haven't made space for people to process, to rest, to grieve. Understanding that has changed how I lead, and how I respond to quiet.

That doesn't mean silence is harmless. It means I can hold it with more compassion—and that care doesn't erase consequences; it clarifies them. It helps me respond without collapsing, without swinging between blame and self-erasure. Because I've been there too—moments when people expected me to speak up, march, show up, fight—and I couldn't. Not because I didn't care. But because I was already stretched thin. Because my nervous system was frayed, and I had nothing left to give. Because I was just one person, trying to become whole after a lifetime of being broken apart.

So now I choose my battles carefully. I speak up when I must. I protect my capacity. I don't shame myself for not carrying everything. That, too, is discernment. That, too, is healing.

This chapter isn't just about telling the truth. It's about knowing which truths to hold, and how. Because not every truth needs to be spoken at full volume to matter. Some truths live in silence. In quiet attention. In choosing to bear witness, without being destroyed by what you see.

That's what happened that day. I walked into a museum and saw the worst of humanity. And then I walked into a restaurant and saw the best. And both were true.

That day in Vietnam reminded me I don't have to take on everything to be a good person—or a healing one. And that lesson didn't just apply to global grief. It applied to my personal life, too. Because there are moments when the most compassionate thing I can do isn't to keep carrying someone—it's to set the relationship down. Even if it hurts. Especially if it's been hurting for a while.

That clarity doesn't always come with anger. Sometimes, it comes with understanding—the realization that someone's doubt wasn't meant to wound you, even if it did. Because not everyone who questions your path is trying to derail it. Some genuinely believe they're being protective. Logical. Grounded. They've seen people struggle, so they try to "warn" you—to be the voice of reason when your dreams sound too big or your timing seems off. Sometimes that comes from love. But other times, those warnings aren't love—they're fear, dressed up as concern.

I spent over a decade in a friendship that held all the contradictions of connection and misalignment. There were seasons of genuine support, both given and received. We met through a shared love of hiking and stayed close through years of change, illness, caregiving, and grief. But over time, our dynamic shifted. Life tugged us in different directions, and the emotional weight between us stopped feeling balanced. Looking back, I think we both stayed longer than we might have if certain circumstances hadn't deepened our mutual dependence. That doesn't diminish the care we shared. But it does help me understand why the relationship eventually became harder to hold.

She often told me how proud she was of me—how amazed she was by the things I'd accomplished. But that praise usually came after the fact. In the moment, when I was about to do something brave—leave a job, travel solo, hike a mountain, start a business—she'd question everything. I always felt like I had to be on guard. Ready to defend myself. Ready to prove I'd thought it all through.

When I entered eating disorder treatment in early 2025, she messaged me often. But treatment was overwhelming. I was confronting trauma, overhauling lifelong behaviors, and trying to survive emotionally while staying nourished. I barely had energy to respond to anyone, including my mother. So I didn't keep her updated on everything—not because I didn't care, but because I couldn't stretch myself any thinner.

When I eventually left treatment—after proving to myself that I could hold the structure on my own—I told her by text. I kept it upbeat, told her I had a lot to share, and that I was feeling great about the decision. I didn't expect celebration. But I didn't expect what came next, either.

She sent a long message back, essentially scolding me. Telling me I had made a mistake. That I needed to go back right away. That I didn't understand how this kind of recovery worked. She didn't ask what I'd learned, what I'd tested, or why I believed I was ready. She didn't listen. She just lectured. She compared me to people who had nothing to do with my story. And without knowing it, she repeated a pattern that had been there for years—she doubted me when I needed someone to trust me most.

I didn't respond. I didn't argue. I didn't send one final text explaining my side or softening the truth. I blocked her. Ten years of friendship ended with a single tap—and even so, it didn't feel impulsive; it felt overdue. I had held that boundary in my body for years. And this moment made it undeniable: I couldn't keep performing strength for someone who only believed in me once I had already proved myself.

Letting go wasn't about punishment. It was about peace. And peace, I realized, meant carrying both grief and grounding: fewer check-ins, fewer shared jokes, a smaller circle—but also a steadier center. I didn't need one more person to explain myself to. I needed room to live.

And sometimes, the need for that space becomes clearest in the subtlest of relationships—the ones that don't feel abusive, but still leave you exhausted. Not because the other person means harm, but because the connection quietly demands more than you have to give.

Sometimes it looks like a follower who praises your vulnerability publicly, but privately expects constant access. Like someone who adores your work, but takes it personally when you don't respond to their DMs. Who sends you long messages you didn't ask for, layered with unspoken expectations. Who assumes your presence online means availability—or worse, obligation.

These moments remind me how blurry the line between connection and consumption can become—especially in digital spaces where emotional intimacy is shared in one direction, but rarely reciprocated with context. It's something every creator, educator, and leader must navigate: how to stay present without becoming emotionally overdrawn.

In the past, I would've replied out of guilt. I would've reshuffled my day to send encouragement, check in, reassure them that they mattered. And it would've felt noble, generous—like I was being the kind of person I once needed. But here's the truth: that version of generosity wasn't resourced. It was rooted in my fear of being seen as selfish. And over time, it eroded my capacity to be present at all.

I've learned to notice that pattern now. When I feel the reflex to overexplain or soften a "no," I ask myself: *Who is this really for?* Is this kindness—or compulsion?

The same questions came up when I ended a collaboration that had once excited me. It had started with alignment, energy, mutual admiration. But slowly, it shifted. Our values began to drift. The dynamic began to take more than it gave. And I found myself dreading every new message—not because of the person, but because of the weight I was carrying just to keep things pleasant.

Ending it felt ungrateful. It also felt necessary. Because I don't believe in burning bridges, but I also don't believe in building new ones from my nervous system. Kindness doesn't obligate me to stay. That's the difference between compassion and self-sacrifice. Between community and codependence. Between being generous—and being drained.

I still care deeply about the people who've supported my work. I still value connection. But I no longer confuse access with intimacy. I can like your post without feeling obligated to reply to your message. I can appreciate your story and still choose not to enter it. That doesn't make me cold. It makes me conscious.

These days, when something feels off, I don't wait until I'm depleted to set a boundary. I move sooner. I don't always offer closure—especially when doing so would cost me mine. Sometimes I go quiet. Not to punish, but to protect. I don't ghost lightly, but I also don't pad my silence with justifications meant to keep me likable. Because past kindness doesn't create future obligation. And love, real love, doesn't ask me to abandon who I am just to be held.

But when you've spent years confusing approval with connection, it can be hard to tell the difference. Sometimes, the ache to be chosen overpowers the instinct to choose yourself. That's what happened with a man who had drifted in and out of my life for many years—someone whose presence always seemed to stir up the part of me that still equated being wanted with being worthy.

It started over 20 years ago. I met him in my early twenties, and I remember being completely taken by his presence—charming, smart, confident, beautiful. He was a bodybuilder, and everything about him seemed polished and powerful. I admired him deeply. But I never kept in touch, not because of anything he did—but because, deep down, I didn't think I was good enough for him. My shame made me retreat before I even gave the connection a chance.

We reconnected again about a decade ago, and once again, I pulled away. It was like clockwork. As soon as things started feeling close, my instinct wasn't to lean in—it was to shrink back. To disappear before I could be fully seen.

So when I reached out again in 2025—after all those years of silence—I thought maybe something had shifted. I was finishing this manuscript, feeling clearer in my body and voice, and something in me wondered: *What would it be like to reconnect from this version of myself?* I didn't expect anything. But when we spoke, he said he was still interested—romantically. And once again, I panicked. Not because I didn't like him. But because I still didn't feel worthy of him.

Only this time, it wasn't just old shame. It was something more complicated—a collision between my instinct to pre-reject myself and a deeper knowing that something didn't feel safe.

I didn't open slowly. I didn't let the connection breathe. I went straight into trauma disclosure. Not to manipulate him, but to manage my own fear. If I told him everything—the eating disorder, the healing work, the years of pain—then at least I'd be in control of the fallout. That's not intimacy. That's self-protection dressed up as transparency.

He didn't respond with empathy. Not really. Instead, he insinuated I might be exaggerating my trauma—that maybe I had built a brand around it, and was now too identified with the pain to see clearly. It was subtle, but it stung. And it made me question my own instinct: Was I sharing all of this to push him away, or was I trying to prove that what I'd been through *really was* as bad as I said? Maybe both.

As we continued talking, he began describing the kind of partner he was looking for—someone who shared his love for self-care and what he called a "shared physical culture," someone with a long history of prioritizing fitness. He didn't say we had to train together, but it was clear that he expected alignment—physically, energetically, and aesthetically. And in that moment, something in me collapsed. I thought about my thirty-year eating disorder. About the years I spent morbidly obese after Stan died. About the degeneration in my spine that now limits how hard I can push myself. I knew, without question, that I could never be what he wanted—and that trying to become it would hurt me. I could already feel myself shrinking. Not just emotionally, but physically—calculating what it would take to be thin enough, fit enough, acceptable enough to be chosen.

That's when I knew I couldn't go forward. I told him directly: we needed to take the idea of a romantic relationship off the table. I expected that to be the end of it; an honest, mature boundary.

But instead of respecting it, he reframed it as rejection. He pivoted quickly into a kind of savior complex—suggesting that maybe this was actually *his role*, to be the man who saved me from myself. That all I needed to do was submit. Trust his masculine leadership. Let him take the reins. My nervous system went on high alert.

It felt like déjà vu—not just from our past, but from so many past experiences with men who believed their control was a form of care. Who thought shaping me was the same as loving me. And in that moment, I didn't just doubt my worth. I doubted my safety.

I ended up muting and archiving our conversations across multiple platforms. Not because I wanted to ghost him or avoid conflict, but because I needed space. My body was clear: this wasn't good for me. Unlike other moments—when the goodbye felt clear and the risk of backlash was low—this was different. With him, it felt like a safety decision. Given his language around submission, my years of abuse by men who wanted the same thing, and the way he reacted when I took a romantic relationship off the table, I didn't want to invite retaliation or backlash. If I had blocked him outright, he would've known. Muting and archiving allowed for quiet distance— the kind that might register to him as silence, but gave me the nervous system protection I needed to stay grounded and out of reach.

What shook me afterward was the question that kept circling: *Had I been pushing him away all these years because I didn't feel worthy? Or had my body always known something that my conscious mind wasn't ready to name?*

The part of me that still wonders if I'm too much—or not enough—isn't broken. She's just remembering. And I'm not abandoning her again.

But walking away didn't erase the ache. Because what I felt with him—that desperate hope that maybe this time, someone would choose all of me—wasn't unique to that moment. It's a pattern I've lived many times before: the rush of possibility, the magnetic pull toward someone who seems powerful, grounded, and just slightly out of reach. It's not really about the man; it's about what he represents. Success. Stability. Safety. The kind of presence I've long believed could validate my worth. And if someone like that truly saw me—all of me— maybe I could finally believe I was lovable.

That's the ache I've been reckoning with. Because it's not just one man. This pattern has echoed before. A spiritual man. A powerful man. A brilliant man. The kind of man I still sometimes believe wouldn't want me if he knew the full truth—all the diagnoses, all the history, all the mess.

So when someone does seem to see me—or when I think they might—I go all in. Headfirst. Heartfirst. Hope-first. I throw my whole self into the possibility of finally being chosen. Even if I barely know them. Even if I'm ignoring red flags. Even if it means I start to disappear.

That's not love. That's starvation. But I'm learning to hold that part of me; the one who still gets swept up in the fantasy. Not to shame her. Not to silence her. But to stay with her. To listen. To guide her back home.

That's what *emotional sobriety* looks like for me right now. Not in the clinical sense—but in the everyday practice of staying grounded in myself, even when my emotions start to surge. It means I don't sprint just because someone lights up my nervous system. I don't confuse intensity with intimacy. I notice the pull without chasing it. I name the ache without handing over the steering wheel. I let the hope rise without letting it run my life. I stay with myself, especially when my old patterns tell me to leave.

But emotional sobriety hasn't just been about staying steady when love lights me up. It's also been about choosing myself quietly, without the need for applause. I used to post about everything I let go of, not to seek praise, but to steady my resolve. If others could affirm that I was doing the right thing, maybe I'd believe it too. But lately, I've been walking away without the post. Letting go without a grand explanation. Choosing myself—not as a song and dance, but as a practice. That's how I know I'm healing.

Even in writing this book, I wrestled with what to include. Not because I'm ashamed, but because I've learned that telling the truth doesn't always mean telling every truth. Integration, for me, is the pause that asks: will sharing this deepen connection, or drain capacity? Some stories are still mine to hold—not out of secrecy, but as an act of healing.

That's a distinction I've had to learn repeatedly, especially in work that centers on transparency. There's a difference between owning your story and monetizing it. Between sharing from wholeness and selling from a wound. I've built much of my work around truth-telling, but I've also learned the hard way that commodifying pain can sometimes recreate the very harm I thought I was healing.

And in the era of content-as-currency, this tension shows up everywhere—in wellness spaces, in social justice circles, in trauma-informed work. We're encouraged to be "authentic," yet rewarded for performance. It creates a dangerous feedback loop where the most visible pain becomes the most validated—where exposure gets mistaken for impact, and storytelling shifts from healing to survival.

It's one thing to share a story because it's ready. It's another to package it because it might perform well. That tension is real, especially for those of us whose stories are part of our work. But visibility without discernment isn't power. It's exposure. And not every truth is meant to be turned into content.

That tension isn't just professional—it's personal. Because the pressure to package pain doesn't always come from a platform. Sometimes, it comes from a person sitting across from you. A partner. A friend. A therapist. Someone who, whether they realize it or not, demands a show of proof before they're willing to offer care.

There were moments in past relationships—one in particular— where I felt like I had to prove my trauma just to be taken seriously. I remember trying to explain my abuse to a Black man who didn't believe white women endured the same kind of trauma as Black women. He wanted qualifiers, comparisons, explicit details—as if pain needed to meet a certain threshold to count. I felt backed into a corner, like my experience didn't carry enough weight on its own. Like I had to amplify my suffering just to be believed.

That's what I mean when I say you shouldn't have to unravel yourself to be believed. I'm not just speaking in metaphor. I'm talking about the emotional stripping people who've experienced trauma are often forced to endure just to receive basic empathy. I'm talking about the cultural and racial narratives that shape who gets to be heard, and who must scream just to matter.

I remember one specific moment that still stings—not because of what I said, but why I said it. That same man asked me to clarify what kind of sexual abuse I'd experienced. And in a moment of desperation, I combined fragments of truth into something I thought might finally land. I said, "Does being assaulted from behind at knifepoint count?" It was true that I'd been assaulted from behind at knifepoint. He came up behind me when I was sixteen, on a quiet road with little traffic. Not a stranger, but a teenage boy from my hometown, just steps from his own house—but it wasn't sexual. At least it never reached that point. I managed to get the knife away and run. Still, in that moment, I offered a distortion. Not to manipulate, but to be taken seriously. I hadn't vocalized most of my traumas to anyone yet. I was thirty-one— still floundering in the aftermath of Stan's death, still trying to stitch myself back together. I didn't have a clear narrative. I had trauma stored in boxes I refused to open; hidden on mental shelves I tried not to look at. I thought if I never unpacked them, maybe they didn't count.

It wouldn't be until my late thirties that I finally assembled my full timeline and saw the truth clearly: I had been sexually violated by eight different men between the ages of nine and nineteen. The first three were family members. So there I was—being expected to justify my right to say I'd been sexually abused, when I hadn't even fully allowed myself to recognize it. At the time, I hadn't named all my abusers. I hadn't mapped out the order of events. I wasn't ready. But I still felt the pressure to offer proof—to shock him into empathy by inflating the story until it felt "valid" enough. Years later, long after we'd broken up, I told him the truth. I told him why I'd said it. That I didn't know how to speak about my trauma without turning up the volume to match his disbelief.

That's the cost of needing to be "believable" more than you're allowed to be human. Of trying to earn care by being broken enough to warrant it. I don't owe anyone the worst parts of me to justify my truth. And neither do you.

That's been one of the hardest lessons of my healing: I don't have to unravel to be seen. I don't have to bleed or break open just to prove I'm in pain. The more I let go of that old script, the one that equated devastation with legitimacy, the more I understand what emotional sobriety actually means.

For most of my life, I thought emotional intensity meant I was alive—that if something didn't consume me, it wasn't real. But now I see that real connection doesn't require collapse. It doesn't ask me to disappear into someone else or perform worthiness to earn love. Emotional sobriety, for me, is the practice of staying steady—of being able to feel the highs and the lows without losing myself in either. It's not about being detached or unaffected. It's about holding my emotions with care instead of letting them carry me away.

That's the shift I'm learning. Not silencing my feelings, but staying rooted while they move through. Responding, not reacting. Choosing, not chasing. That's what healing looks like now. Not a lack of emotion, but a deeper trust in my ability to hold it.

There was a time when my body's response felt like an emergency. When any spark of possibility made me want to sprint—toward love, toward safety, toward someone who might finally make me feel enough. But now, I'm learning how to pause. To let the spark exist without needing to set my whole life on fire.

I don't want to live at the mercy of the next man who feels "safe enough." I want to be available for love without abandoning myself to get it. I want to feel attraction without needing it to mean everything. And I want to let people show me who they are, over time, instead of assuming that chemistry equals capacity. That's what I mean when I say I'm integrating. I'm not just seeing my patterns. I'm shifting how I respond to them.

And no, I'm not perfect at it. Sometimes I still spiral. Sometimes I still fall. But I catch myself faster now. I soothe, rather than shame. I return, rather than run.

But before I got there—before I could even begin to sort through what happened—I had to sit with the ache I was still carrying. Because it wasn't just about one man or one moment. It was about the deeper story I've long attached to being chosen—the idea that being loved by someone outwardly composed, successful, or impressive might finally silence the voice inside me that still wonders if I'm too much, or not enough. That ache didn't start with the man who recently reappeared in my life. But his presence brought it to the surface—and gave me a chance to face it with more honesty than I ever have before.

That ache wasn't new. It had shown up before—with other men, in other places, under different names. But the pattern was the same: the moment someone seemed to meet my fantasy of a safe, powerful, emotionally intelligent partner, I collapsed into hope. I threw my whole self into the possibility that this could finally be it. That someone might see me—all of me—and still stay.

That wasn't love. That was longing masquerading as proof. And that's what I'm learning to hold now. Not to shame myself for it. But to recognize it as a survival reflex—a pattern born of emptiness, not alignment. To pause before I give away all my power. To tell myself: yes, you are worthy of love, and you don't have to abandon yourself to earn it.

That's how I knew I was shifting. Because even though the old ache was still there—even though part of me wanted to throw myself into the fantasy—another part of me stepped forward. The part that could say, "Not this time." The part that could choose space, grounding, reflection. The part that could remember: if love makes me smaller, it's not love.

But that pattern—the belief that I had to prove my worth by pushing past my limits—didn't just show up in relationships. It showed up in my healing too. Especially in my body.

I used to chase healing the way I chased love: through performance. Through proving. If I could just endure more, do more, climb higher—maybe then I'd be worthy of rest. Maybe then I'd be strong enough to deserve peace.

That mindset followed me into the mountains. I threw myself into hiking full tilt, determined to conquer something inside myself by conquering summits outside me. It didn't matter how much my body hurt—in fact, the pain became part of the story. My knees screamed. My spine throbbed. But overriding my body made me feel powerful. I'd learned early on to ignore its signals, and part of me still believed that pain was something to outrun.

So when I started to slow down—not by choice, but by necessity— I didn't know how to hold it. The pain wasn't just physical anymore. It became emotional. I grieved not being able to keep up. I hated that Everest would always be out of reach. I felt like a failure for not being strong enough to bypass the very pain that had once made me feel invincible.

That grief stayed with me until August 2024, when I saw the scans: my L5 vertebra shrinking, almost no disc space between L5 and S1, spinal stenosis, scoliosis. I'd taught anatomy and physiology for years—I didn't need a doctor to interpret it. I knew in an instant what it meant.

Still, I asked. During a telehealth visit, I found myself asking if this meant I'd have to give up high-altitude mountaineering. My doctor's face shifted—a quick flash of disbelief, softened just as fast by kindness when she saw I was holding back tears. "For the foreseeable future, Stephanie," she said gently.

That moment changed something. Not because she said it, but because I finally heard it. I wasn't weak. I wasn't giving up. I was listening. For the first time, I wasn't trying to override my body. I was trying to honor it.

Even so, I couldn't bring myself to let go of my gear right away. Thousands of dollars in high-altitude mountaineering equipment sat untouched—relics of a dream I wasn't ready to bury. Every pack, every crampon, every piece of gear whispered a familiar promise: *You're not done yet.* I kept telling myself that maybe, if I trained hard enough— if I built enough lean muscle around the damage—I could still protect what was broken. Not heal it, not undo it, but shield it. Compensate for it. Pretend it didn't matter.

It wasn't just hope. It was survival logic. Accomplishing had been my lifeline for so long—proof that I was strong, capable, unshatterable. Letting go of Everest didn't just mean letting go of a dream; it meant admitting I have limits. And for someone who once survived by outperforming pain, that admission carried shame.

But when I decided to sell and donate everything and pursue full-time travel in 2025, I knew: I couldn't carry the weight of an old identity into this new life. Letting go of that gear wasn't just logistical. It was a turning point. I cried packing crampons I'll never need, then felt my shoulders drop—a body-level yes to a life that no longer requires proof. A quiet, powerful moment of truth: *I don't have to accomplish to be enough. I don't have to keep pushing through pain to earn my healing.*

The mountains taught me many things. But maybe the most important was this: healing doesn't always come through effort. Sometimes it comes through stillness. Through listening. Through honoring the signals of a body that's been trying to speak all along.

That realization didn't land all at once. Like most truths, it came in layers—over years of misinterpreting stillness as failure, and effort as proof of worth. Healing has never been a linear process for me. There were times when I thought I had "failed" simply because I wasn't ready to sit with what was surfacing. But readiness isn't a measure of worth; it's a measure of nervous system capacity. And I didn't understand that until much later.

Mindfulness, like healing, isn't a fixed ritual. It's a relationship. There are seasons when I meditate daily, move with breath, and journal every emotion. And there are seasons when showing up looks like getting out of bed and noticing I'm still here. I used to judge the shifts; to assume I'd lost progress when my tools changed. But now I understand every tool has a season. That the things that saved me once aren't always the things that serve me now. And that letting go of an old practice isn't regression. It's responsiveness.

That's the wisdom I've drawn from my study of yoga—not just the poses, but the philosophy. Especially the idea that practice itself is a living thing. That discipline doesn't mean rigidity. It means devotion. And devotion, for me, means listening: to my body, to my timing, to my truth.

So when I say I'm healing, I don't mean I've arrived. I mean I'm attuning. I'm learning to respect the pace my body and soul can actually hold. I'm learning to trust the part of me that whispers, "You're ready now, but it's okay that you weren't before." And I'm learning that what counts isn't how consistently I show up with one particular tool—it's how gently I return to myself when I've drifted away.

That's what healing looks like for me now—not just in practice, but in discernment. In learning to pause before I speak, to check whether what I'm sharing is rooted in connection or in fear. I'm still learning how to tell the difference between disclosure and self-abandonment. Between connection and reenactment. Between intuition and avoidance. But one thing I do know now is this: love—in any form—should not ask me to shrink. Not for a man. Not for an ideal. Not even for the version of myself I used to be. If love demands I silence my body, override my truth, or disappear to be accepted, then it's not love. Whether it's the love of another or the love of myself, it must make room for all of me—not just the parts that feel easy to hold.

Still, even with that clarity, I sometimes find myself spiraling—especially when old wounds get triggered in new ways. When that happens, I've learned to reach for the people who know how to hold space without needing to fix me. People who reflect me back to myself instead of reshaping me into someone easier to understand. That's what happened recently, after a moment that left me questioning whether I was honoring my truth or simply reenacting my past. I brought all of it to David.

He's known me long enough to recognize the difference between when I'm naming my truth and when I'm unraveling inside it. I told him about what happened with the man I'd recently reconnected with—someone I once admired deeply, and who had resurfaced just as I was finishing this manuscript. I shared the shame, the doubt, the way my boundaries were twisted into a spiritual test, and how quickly I collapsed into hope. How I shared too much, too fast—not out of trust, but as a preemptive defense. And how afterward, I couldn't tell whether I'd been pushing someone away, or trying to prove I was still worthy of being held.

David didn't flinch. He never does. He didn't offer fixes or strategies. Just presence. And then, in his grounded way, he said: "You've overcome so much. You have so much to be proud of. If someone can't see that, it's their problem. Not yours."

It didn't land like reassurance. It landed like truth. Like a reset. Because I've spent most of my life around mirrors that distorted me—people who needed me to be smaller, softer, simpler to love me. But David has always reflected something else: my wholeness.

At one point, while I was still spinning about men who'd tried to reshape or "guide" me—who offered feedback I didn't ask for, or held affection hostage to improvement—I told him how those experiences had chipped away at me. How they still whisper, *Maybe you're too much. Maybe you need to change.* And he just said, with that steady clarity I've come to rely on: "Just do Stephanie."

It was such a simple phrase, but it cut through everything. He wasn't offering advice—he never does. He was holding a mirror. Not the kind that shrinks you, but the kind that helps you return to yourself.

That's what safe love does. It doesn't mold you. It mirrors you—gently, without agenda. It reminds you that being seen doesn't start with someone who desires you. It starts with someone who doesn't need anything from you to reflect your truth.

The more I heal, the more I've come to understand that discernment isn't silence—it's sovereignty. It's the ability to feel the urge to overexplain or overshare, and still choose presence over panic. It's asking: *Am I sharing to connect, or to survive?* And having the courage to pause when the answer isn't clear.

For most of my life, I thought vulnerability required full access. That if I wasn't telling the whole story, I was being dishonest. But now I know: some truths don't need an audience. Some parts of me are sacred. Some parts are mine to hold, or to offer only to those who can meet them with care. David reminded me of that. Not with a lecture, but with quiet conviction. A phrase. A mirror.

Because the people we share our stories with become mirrors. And for too long, I only saw my shame reflected back at me. But now, I choose different mirrors. Safe ones. Ones that remind me I'm not too much, and I don't have to contort myself to be worthy of love. That's peace. That's discernment. That's what I'm learning to trust.

Still, that discernment took time. There was a chapter in my life when I hadn't yet learned the difference between being seen and being centered—when storytelling became a way to feel significant. I'd share things that weren't mine to share; gossip dressed as insight. I'd inflate my role in certain moments to sound more central, more wounded, more wise. Not out of malice, but out of a desperate hunger to be seen.

Sometimes I still feel the old pull: the desire to make a story sharper or sadder than it was. Not because I'm dishonest—but because I learned, early on, that drama made people listen. That it made me feel valuable. That it gave me something to offer when I didn't believe I was enough on my own.

Gossip gave me power I didn't think I had. Embellishment gave me shape when I felt invisible. But both came at a cost—usually to my integrity, and sometimes to someone's trust.

These days, I catch myself. I feel the urge to puff up or shrink down, and I pause. I remind myself: I don't need to put pain or power on display. I don't need to impress anyone. I just need to stay honest—even when honesty feels small.

I used to think if people weren't looking at me, I didn't exist. But gossip isn't intimacy. And being the center of attention isn't the same as being held.

That's the work now: to stay real without reaching. To tell the truth without twisting it. To trust that the quiet version of me—the one who doesn't need to be the most interesting person in the room—is still enough.

I still love sharing stories. Part of why I pursue grand adventures is because I cherish the meaning they hold—and yes, I love the way they captivate a room. But I try to be mindful now. I ask more questions. I listen more closely. When someone shares something they're proud of, especially in front of others, I try not to follow it with a story that outshines them just for the sake of standing out.

I don't always get it right. My ego still flares up. But I try not to be too hard on myself. That instinct to put on a show was a survival strategy. And it didn't come from nowhere—I grew up in a culture where gossip was currency, where being interesting was a kind of protection. Of course I learned to survive that way.

But survival isn't the same as alignment. And these days, I'm learning how to stay true without needing to be loud to feel seen.

That clarity has been hard-won. For a long time, I didn't understand that truth-telling could include restraint. I thought I had to tell the whole story or none of it. If I didn't include every detail—where it happened, when, why—then I believed I wasn't being fully transparent. But that wasn't honesty. That was trauma logic. That was my nervous system trying to find safety through control, as if I could preempt shame by leaving nothing unsaid.

Black-and-white thinking has been one of my oldest survival tools. It made the world feel more predictable. If I was all in, I was good. If I held back, I was hiding. If someone praised me, I was lovable. If they pulled away, I was worthless. These binaries gave me structure when the world didn't feel safe, but they also kept me stuck in a cycle where I only felt alive when I was being extreme.

That mindset followed me into how I told my story. I thought visibility required exposure. That honesty had to be complete, uncensored, sometimes even shocking. I believed authenticity didn't count unless it came with receipts. But now I understand that healing doesn't live in extremes; it lives in nuance. It lives in the both/and. I can be honest without overexplaining. I can protect someone's privacy and still stand in my truth. I can speak from the scar instead of the wound. That doesn't make me dishonest. It makes me discerning.

This didn't click overnight. It took years of writing, coaching, and being misread. Years of learning what happened when I shared too much, too soon, with people who hadn't earned the right to hear it. I thought I was being transparent, but often I was bleeding on command. It took friends like David to remind me that sovereignty over my story isn't secrecy; it's wisdom. And it took noticing how often I asked myself whether holding back meant I was being fake. I had to learn that not everyone is safe. That not everything needs to be said out loud. That truth doesn't require documentation to be valid.

That belief—that realness means rawness—traces all the way back to Chapter 1, when I wrote about believing my pain had to be undeniable to be taken seriously. I thought every trauma had to be spelled out in full detail or it wouldn't count. That was the performance of proof—the self-betrayal dressed as courage. But real transparency, the kind I'm learning now, doesn't ask me to strip myself bare just to be seen. It asks something quieter: the courage to hold something sacred, even when no one else knows it's there.

This is what it means for me to live in the gray. It's the middle ground between collapse and control, between silence and oversharing. It's where discernment lives. Where truth becomes less about performance and more about permission—the permission to share from a place of choice, not panic. That shift matters—not just for me, but for the people I serve. I used to model overdisclosure as a way to build connection. But now I know that connection built on overexposure isn't true safety. It's a survival bond.

These days, I ask myself before sharing: *What am I hoping this disclosure will give me? And more importantly: Do I already have that within myself?* If the answer is no—if I'm hoping it will give me validation, permission, or safety—then I pause. I exhale. I listen. Not to the pressure, but to the part of me that's finally learning what freedom feels like.

That's what this whole chapter is about: learning to stay real without tearing yourself open to prove it. Learning to say, "This is mine," even when I choose not to say it out loud. That's the new kind of honesty I'm learning to trust. Because transparency without safety isn't bravery. It's re-traumatization. And I'm not performing my pain anymore. I'm owning my truth—gently, wisely, and on my own terms.

That shift didn't just affect what I shared; it shaped how I viewed the entire project. Because even as I wrote these pages with clarity and depth, I hesitated to name what they truly were. I tiptoed around the obvious, unsure if I had "earned" the right to say it out loud.

It took longer than I'd like to admit to call this book what it is: a memoir. Not because it wasn't clear. The structure was personal. The voice was intimate. The stories were raw and rooted in memory. But still, I kept hesitating—sidestepping the label like it was too bold, too exposed, too presumptuous.

My earlier books had memoir elements, but they were always wrapped in "how-to" guidance. Blended with tools and techniques. Framed as personal growth. As if my story alone wasn't enough to help people—as if it had to be educational to be worthy of space on someone's shelf.

That wasn't just about preference. It was about palatability. Institutions—publishers, programs, platforms—often value personal stories more when they come with lessons. As if narrative alone can't hold worth unless it's distilled into digestible takeaways.

This time, there's no curriculum. No worksheets. No bulleted lists or step-by-step takeaways. Just my story. My truth. My voice, unbraided from performance. And naming it plainly—*memoir*— still feels risky.

Because naming it opens the door to all the questions I've spent a lifetime trying not to hear. *Who do you think you are? Why would anyone care? What makes your story worth reading?*

Those questions don't come from logic. They come from old wounds. From being a little girl who was told she was nothing and was made to feel invisible. From growing up in spaces where being seen came with a cost. Where sharing too much got you punished, and holding back meant you were lying. From being told that survival wasn't special unless you turned it into something palatable.

But I'm not writing this for applause. I'm writing this because I need to. Because this—this naming—is part of the healing.

I've worked hard to untangle my worth from achievement. From productivity. From being useful. And yet, here I was, clinging to the belief that unless this book taught something concrete, it wouldn't count. That unless it followed a step-by-step model, it wouldn't help anyone. That my story, by itself, wasn't enough. But that's not true. My story is the help.

It's the kind of help I once needed and couldn't find. Not because others weren't trying—but because they filtered their stories through too many disclaimers, too many layers of safety, too much smoothing of the edges. They left out the parts that would've made me feel less alone.

I don't want to do that anymore. I don't want to package my truth in a way that protects people from how real it is—or protects me from how it might land. I want to tell it whole, even if it's imperfect. Even if it's messy. Even if it doesn't come with a conclusion tied in a bow.

Because the point of this book isn't to instruct. It's to witness. To trace the arc of what it means to live *see through*— to be visible without being swallowed. To tell the truth without telling it all. To hold the paradox of shame and pride, fear and clarity, grief and agency—and say, *This is still mine.*

So yes, this is a memoir. And no, I don't have to apologize for that. I don't have to earn it by suffering harder or spelling it out more clearly. I don't have to turn myself into a teacher to be trusted. I can be the student and the story. I can be the mirror and the mess.

Naming this book a memoir isn't about ego. It's about reclamation. Choosing that label is ownership on the page—not more exposure, just steadier authorship. It's not a claim to fame. It's a commitment to truth. It's saying to that younger version of me—the one who was told she had nothing to say: *Look at us now. We are telling it all, gently. Not to be famous—but to be free.* Because for so long, we believed that being seen by the world was the only way to prove we mattered. That recognition would rescue us from invisibility. But we don't need rescuing anymore. We're not writing for validation. We're writing to reclaim space. To honor the girl who was told she was nothing, and to show her she was always enough.

That reclamation didn't stop with storytelling. It reached into how I defined success, too. For a long time, I believed my accomplishments only counted if I carried them alone—that self-made meant self-worthy. Asking for help felt like weakness. Ease felt like cheating. I couldn't call myself successful unless I had suffered to get there. But that wasn't ambition; that was trauma talking.

So when I began using ChatGPT to help me structure this book—not to write it for me, but to reflect things back, help me think more clearly, and organize what I already knew—I wrestled. Not just with the technology, but with myself. Would people think I cheated? That I didn't really write it? Would they disqualify everything I'd poured into these pages if they knew I'd received help clarifying the flow?

But staying silent about how I got here felt like another kind of pretending. And this book is about choosing honesty, even when it challenges convention. So yes, I used tools. And no, that doesn't make this story any less mine.

What's wild is that I coach people through this kind of sabotage all the time. I've had clients minimize their growth the moment it got easier. I've seen students discount their success the second it started to feel less hard. We're so conditioned to equate struggle with legitimacy—to believe that if we didn't crawl our way there, we haven't earned the right to stand tall.

But here's what I know now: great creators receive support. Great leaders collaborate. Great visionaries delegate what drains them—not because they're lazy, but because they understand the cost of misusing their energy.

While writing this book, I also released a new trauma healing toolkit, and I also felt like a failure then. Not because there was evidence to support that feeling—but because my nervous system couldn't yet distinguish between rest and rejection, between help and inadequacy. That's how quickly imposter syndrome shows up—not as a rational assessment, but as a reflex to keep you small.

And that reflex doesn't just live in our work. It lives in our voice. Our visibility. Our willingness to admit what's true. And the only way I know to challenge it—to rewrite it—is to name it in real time. So that's what this is. A naming. A refusal to let shame dictate the terms of what gets to count.

I didn't write this book by myself. But I did write it. I didn't write it in isolation. But the stories, the meanings, the message—they're mine. And if that truth is clearer, stronger, and more organized because I allowed myself to receive support? That's not disqualifying. That's what healing makes possible.

Because a previous version of me would've never allowed this. I would've agonized over what people might think. I would've hidden the truth about how I got here, not because I was being dishonest, but because I didn't feel strong enough to survive someone questioning it. If someone had called me out—if they'd said, *You didn't write this on your own*— I think my knees would've buckled under the shame.

That's how deep the conditioning runs. We're taught to prove our worth through suffering. To equate independence with strength. To see asking for help as weakness, even though—and I know this not just emotionally, but scientifically—it's not how we're built. I taught biology for years. I taught evolution. And one of the truths that never stopped humbling me was this: humans are deeply social creatures. We're wired for interdependence. Our survival has always hinged on connection—on shared labor, shared knowledge, shared care.

So how did we get here? How did we learn to believe that we're supposed to do it all alone? That needing support makes us less worthy of success, less deserving of recognition, less *real*? I don't have all the answers. But I know this belief nearly drowned me.

Because I've spent most of my life struggling to keep my head above water—not just from trauma, but from the isolation I felt trying to survive it on my own. I didn't know how to reach for help. I thought needing support made me a burden. I thought being strong meant staying silent about what I needed. And it's only now, after years of unlearning, that I can say this with conviction: we're not meant to do this alone.

So I'll name my truth here—not as a defense, but as an offering. I received support while writing this book. And I needed it. And I'm still proud of what I've created. If anything, I'm proud *because* I was willing to be supported. Because I finally reached out my arm. Because I let myself be held.

And if sharing that makes one other person feel less ashamed about needing help, then it's not just part of the process. It's part of the purpose. Because support doesn't always look the way we expect it to. Sometimes it comes through collaboration, reflection, or shared labor. Other times, it comes in the form of a little white pill—a bridge between surviving and not. I've received help in many forms over the years. And some of the most life-saving arrived during the moments when I could barely hold myself up.

I didn't start taking medication until my mid-twenties. And when I did, it wasn't some gentle transition into support—it was during a time when I was completely unraveling. I was bingeing and purging daily. I was having recurring thoughts of not wanting to be here. My nervous system was flooded, and I didn't have the tools—or the bandwidth—to process anything I was carrying. Medication wasn't an enhancement. It was a last resort. It helped me stay functional at a time when I didn't feel safe inside my own skin.

Because I started taking medication at such a critical low point, I internalized the belief that I needed it to survive. That without it, I would collapse. I've held onto that association for years—that if I wasn't medicated, I couldn't be trusted with my own mind. That if I stopped taking something, I would fall apart. That if I was stable, it must be the pills. Not the work. Not the healing. Not me. But I knew in my heart that wasn't true. I just wanted to prove it to myself.

Prozac was the most recent medication I was on, but it wasn't my first. Over the past twenty years, I've tried a variety of SSRIs, trying to find the one that made me feel less unstable, less tired, less unsafe in my own brain. Some helped. Some made things worse. Some simply numbed everything. But all of them became tangled up in the same belief: this is what's keeping me functional. And maybe that was true back then. But what if it's not true anymore?

For the first time, I'm in a very different environment. I'm not in a toxic job. I'm not drowning in overwork. I'm not ignoring my needs to meet someone else's expectations. I'm finally in a chapter of life where I've created space—not just for rest, but for regulation. I've built a rhythm I can control. I've chosen work that aligns with my values. And I'm listening more carefully to myself than I ever have before.

Over the past few months, I tapered off Prozac slowly and responsibly, tracking sleep, mood, and breath the way I once tracked miles. With each decrease in dosage, I paid close attention not because I was afraid, but because I cared. I wanted to know what my body actually felt like without being filtered through a drug meant to keep me from feeling too much. I wanted to meet myself without the noise, without the dulling, without the disconnect. And now, here I am, meeting her for the very first time. I am so proud of her. I can feel a new level of love and admiration for her I'd never known before.

And I want to pause here to say this clearly: I'm not anti-medication. I'm not suggesting that anyone should stop taking theirs, especially not without support. Medication can be life-saving. It was for me. And for many people, it's an essential part of stability and survival. My decision to taper wasn't impulsive or uninformed. I drew on years of research, my background in anatomy and physiology, and the tools I've built to regulate what once drowned me. I've invested hours in self-reflection, therapy, and trauma healing. This isn't proof—it's practice: testing who I am now, with more tools and more room to self-regulate. It's about discovering who I am underneath the scaffolding that once held me up.

And what I'm learning is this: hard isn't the same as dangerous. Fatigue isn't the same as dysfunction. Intensity isn't the same as instability. I still have moments where I feel the tightness in my chest. Where I wonder if I'm okay. But I also notice that I don't spiral in the same way I used to. I don't collapse. I pause. I reflect. I care for myself in ways that weren't accessible to me twenty years ago.

I used to think medication was the only thing that kept me upright. But now I can see that what's keeping me steady is actually the work I've done. The tools I've built. The space I've created to feel without drowning. To remember without disappearing. To rest without shame. This isn't regression. It's reclamation.

I didn't do this because I needed to prove that I could survive without medication. I did it because I wanted to meet the version of myself that existed underneath it. I wanted to know who I was when I wasn't sedated, overstimulated, overworked, or overperforming. Not because I believe healing requires suffering, but because I believe it requires honesty. And I don't think I've ever had the chance to know what my honest baseline even feels like.

Maybe for the first time in my life, I'm meeting myself without the trauma, without the pills, without the performance. Not because I've transcended anything. But because I've finally slowed down enough to listen. And what I'm hearing isn't collapse. It's clarity.

Telling the truth without telling it all doesn't mean hiding how you got here. Sometimes the most honest thing you can say is: *I didn't do this alone—and that doesn't make it less mine.*

Because this isn't a story about being fully healed. It's a story about being human—about making room for nuance, for quiet knowing, for the truths that don't need an audience to be real.

And yet, even now—with all that I've learned—there are moments when I still doubt myself. When I wonder if I'm too much, or not enough. When someone misreads my boundaries, my voice, my stillness… and I feel the old ache rise.

That's where we're headed next—not into collapse, but into the tender terrain of being misunderstood and misread. Not broken, but finally ready to see it differently.

See Through Reflections

1. Personal Reflection

- When have you shared more than you were ready to—not out of connection, but out of fear you wouldn't be believed? What did it cost you, and what did it protect?

- Is there a story you've told so many times that it no longer feels like yours? What would it mean to reclaim it—or let it rest without explanation?

- What parts of you feel most true when they remain unspoken? Can you trust that silence can also be self-respect?

2. Group or Cultural Exploration

- In the spaces you belong to (professional, relational, digital), when is vulnerability celebrated? When is it commodified or rewarded for performance rather than presence?

- How have the systems you've moved through (education, publishing, activism, wellness) shaped the way you tell your story—and whose comfort that story serves?

- What would collective care look like in a space where boundaries were honored as deeply as disclosures, and where safety wasn't dependent on constant sharing?

3. Somatic/Embodied Practice

- Think of a time you felt pressured to "prove" your pain—through detail, urgency, or performance. Where in your body did that pressure live?

- Place a hand on that space. Breathe. Say softly, "I don't have to unravel to be real." Let the words land. Let them loosen your grip on the need to explain. Stay with yourself.

Chapter 6
Misunderstood, Not Broken

There comes a point in healing when you stop asking, "What's wrong with me?" and start asking, "What's wrong with the places that keep calling me broken?" That shift doesn't always feel triumphant. Sometimes it feels like grief—waking to the quiet knowing that the people, programs, or professions you hoped would save you can't. Or worse, that they might hurt you in new ways. When you've spent years trying to prove you're worthy of support, it can feel radical to wonder whether the support itself is safe.

And that question isn't only personal; it's systemic. What does it say about our institutions when the very environments built to offer care can replicate the same harms they claim to heal? We see it clearly in mental health care—where pain is often filtered through a framework before it's fully witnessed, and where healing sometimes hinges on how well you're understood.

For almost two decades, I tried to convince myself that therapy could feel safe, even when it rarely did. Not because I didn't want help, but because I didn't want my pain reduced to a billing code that matched someone else's definition of brokenness. I still believe in therapy because of the few therapists I've met who were kind, attuned, and skillful. But those few have been the exception, and holding onto them has been difficult against the weight of all the times I was hurt in spaces that were supposed to help me heal.

There's something uniquely shattering about being dismissed when you're already raw. When you're already doing the vulnerable work of saying, "This is what I've been through," only to have it reduced to a formula, a diagnosis, or worse—a judgment.

I once told my first therapist at 25—the one I started seeing just before Stan died—that I wasn't particularly religious. That I had spent most of my life feeling like God had abandoned me during the years I was being abused. Everything was unraveling all at once. I had just begun talking about my childhood trauma. I had just started my PhD program. Stan's mom had died. Then Stan died. Then I closed on the house we were supposed to move into together. It all happened in less than two months. I was shattered. And instead of meeting me in that grief, she said I would never heal unless I accepted God into my life.

Another therapist called me an asshole—not in jest, but as a response to something I shared about a common trauma response of mine: pulling away when I felt overwhelmed. I was trying to explain that I sometimes went silent not because I didn't care, but because I cared so deeply that I was afraid I couldn't meet people's needs. His response? "Sounds like you're just being an asshole."

Then there was the one in 2023 who told me I was damaged. I had opened up about how frustrating it was that trauma still lived in my body. That even after years of work, I still felt it in waves of sadness, moments of collapse, lingering pain. I wasn't asking to be fixed—I just wanted to be witnessed. And her response was, "Well, what do you expect, Stephanie? You're damaged."

That phrase stayed with me. Not because it was true, but because it echoed something I had feared my whole life—that no matter how far I came, I would always be seen as broken.

But the most jarring experience came in 2025, when I entered an eating disorder recovery program after thirty years of fighting that battle on my own. I had done the brave thing—shared the full history, even the parts from my teens and twenties that no longer reflected who I was but were still part of the journey. Within thirty minutes of meeting me, the psychiatrist wanted to diagnose me as bipolar. I challenged it, calmly: "You've only known me for half an hour." And she said, without hesitation, "I'm also taking information from your chart and background." Which meant she had already made the decision before she'd even met me.

What she was really saying was this: the version of me that struggled as a teenager—the one who was being abused and grasping for anything to survive—was enough to label me for life. She didn't see that the so-called instability in my twenties came after I found my partner dead and was addressing trauma for the first time. She didn't see where I was now. She saw my survival and called it pathology.

And it didn't stop there. On the day I left the program—just hours before I walked away for good—I was sitting on a couch in group therapy, sharing a hard-earned win. I had followed my meal plan, kept myself safe, and done what I said I would do. I was proud, and I said so. I sat there, steady and smiling, while naming the progress I had fought for.

And that's when the therapist said it: "I'm worried this might be a manic episode." Right there. In front of the group.

That moment made the decision for me. I had been questioning the program for weeks, but that response—that refusal to see me clearly—was the breaking point. I realized then that staying wasn't just unhelpful. It was harmful.

This wasn't an isolated misunderstanding. It was the culmination of a slow erosion—a pattern I had seen unfold as soon as I started advocating for myself. I had made it clear from early on that I didn't think the program was a good fit. Not because I didn't need support—I did—but because I knew my healing couldn't happen in an environment that didn't trust me to know myself. I told them I wasn't claiming to be "better," just that I wanted to do the work in a space that felt like care, not harm.

The more vocal I became about their assessments and their inability to meet me with nuance, the more convinced they became that I was the problem. They interpreted my self-awareness as instability. My voice as volatility. And as their doubt grew louder, so did my resolve.

So I created my own structure. My own tests. Part of it was defiance—I was tired of not being seen, of always having to be strong when what I wanted was to let go, to stop bracing for battle. But it was also integration turned practical—putting what I know about my body into a plan I could trust. I followed the plan. I proved I could hold my recovery outside the confines of their system. And when I showed up that day, proud and grounded, ready to name what I had accomplished, they didn't celebrate it. They labeled it.

She tried to walk it back, of course. Said she was just concerned. That maybe my "overconfidence" would lead me to think I was fine when I wasn't. That I might relapse once the high wore off. But the subtext was clear: my joy made her uneasy. My pride looked suspicious. My clarity was framed as dangerous.

After we finished sharing, we moved into an exercise using a set of illustrated images often used in therapy to explore inner parts—visual metaphors for the sub-personalities that show up in different moments. The therapist asked us to choose the one that best represented who was present in us right then. I picked two.

The first was a woman in a flowing white dress, arms lifted, birds and flowers circling her like a celebration. She looked joyful. Free. I told the group: this is the part of me you saw when I spoke—the one who felt proud of what I had done and wanted to name it out loud. That's the part I wish could lead more often. The one who still believes, somewhere deep down, that peace is possible.

But I also picked a second card: a figure fully encased in metal armor, helmet to boots, weapon drawn and shield raised. He was ready for battle. And I told them, as calmly and clearly as I could: this part is always with me. He never leaves.

Because this is what happens when joy gets punished. When confidence gets misread as mania. When the very systems that are supposed to help you heal become places where you must stay armored just to protect your spirit.

This pattern plays out in schools and workplaces, and—as you've seen in earlier chapters—in meetings, monasteries, and sanctuaries. Authenticity is applauded right up until it challenges the unspoken rules, until it becomes too loud, too real, too inconvenient.

As a woman—and especially as someone who's endured and rebuilt after trauma—I've learned that pride doesn't always read as integration. Sometimes, it reads as arrogance. Or delusion. Or danger. The same clarity that might be praised in someone else becomes a red flag when it comes from someone like me. And that's not just personal—it's cultural. We're taught to reward vulnerability only when it's soft, palatable, and self-doubting. Not when it stands tall. Not when it dares to feel proud.

That's what made the moment in group therapy so defining. I said to them—out loud, in that moment—that what they had just witnessed was a live demonstration of what it means to move through the world as someone who's been harmed by helpers. First, the joyful girl spoke. Then, the armored one had to step in. Not because I was delusional. Not because I was unstable. But because I've learned, over and over again, that even in spaces of so-called care, I might not be safe.

Those two parts of me—the free one and the fighter—are always in tension. One wants to exhale. The other stays alert. And what I needed that day wasn't another label. I needed to be seen. Both of me. All of me. But they couldn't do that. And I couldn't stay.

Instead of honoring my growth, they tried to shrink me back down. Instead of meeting my joy with presence, they met it with suspicion. Instead of seeing my pride as a sign of integration, they called it a risk.

That moment crystallized something I had felt my whole life: When I'm proud, people call me unstable. When I'm clear, they call me arrogant. When I speak, they call me dangerous.

This is the legacy of being labeled instead of listened to. Of having PTSD or nervous system dysregulation mistaken for madness. Of having ambition—especially in a woman, especially in someone shaped by survival—pathologized instead of honored.

So yes, there are reasons I'm hesitant to go to therapy. Not because I think I'm above support, but because I've too often had to protect myself within systems that were supposed to protect me. Many people enter the field because of their own pain. Some transform that pain into safety for others; some pass the wound along. And when those wounds go unexamined, they don't just stay hidden—they get projected onto the very people most in need of care.

The system doesn't help either. If you want therapy covered by insurance, you usually need a diagnosis. Your humanity must be coded. Your pain must be justified. And if you start to get better, you risk losing access to care. Healing becomes a liability.

It's not that I don't believe in therapy. I do. But I also believe this: I don't need to be fixed. I need to be met. For me, discernment means knowing how and where that happens—what I share, what I hold, and which rooms have earned access to my truth. I want to sit in front of someone who sees my insight not as a mask, but as a survival strategy. Who understands that complexity isn't a symptom; it's a sign of wholeness. Who knows that sometimes the most dangerous thing you can do to someone finally starting to believe in herself is to pathologize her power.

The deeper harm wasn't just what they said. It was what they missed. They saw symptoms. I saw survival. And that's a difference that changes everything.

Because "symptoms" language—as clinical as it sounds—can be a form of social control. It centers compliance over context. It flattens people's stories into checkboxes. It strips away the why behind the what. In many therapeutic settings—especially those tied to insurance or institutional systems—care begins with an intake form. A checklist. A diagnosis. You're asked to describe your thoughts, behaviors, and emotions not as parts of a larger story, but as symptoms to be categorized. And once those symptoms are named, they can shape how everything else is seen.

This model can help in some cases, but it can also make healing about fitting a mold rather than being understood. It reinforces a dangerous idea: that healing should look one way. That any deviation from the norm—any disruption, grief, protest, or fire—must be contained. Or worse, corrected. It asks, "How can we manage this person?" instead of, "What has this person survived?"

And this gap isn't limited to therapy rooms. In boardrooms, classrooms, and congregations, people are still being misread through biased frameworks—punished for their trauma responses instead of met with curiosity.

I used to think that if I told the truth clearly enough, people would get it. That if I spoke openly, bravely, and with the kind of nuance that left no room for misunderstanding, they would understand. But the truth is, some people don't want understanding. They want a version of reality that feels familiar, that makes sense to them, even if it erases you. They want your story to match their script, their diagnosis, their comfort. And when it doesn't, they don't just reject the story—they reject you.

And sometimes, the hurt goes even deeper. Because there's a particular kind of heartbreak that comes when your vulnerability is not just dismissed, but weaponized.

One moment from eating disorder treatment still lingers in my memory. We were sitting around a lunch table, casually chatting about one of the art projects we'd been assigned. I made a light comment—something about not having finished mine yet. I wasn't looking for advice or critique. But one therapist smirked and said, "Maybe one day you'll finish something."

It landed like a slap. Heat rose to my face, my jaw locked, my chest tightened. What was meant as a joke exposed the exact wound I was fighting to heal—the fear that no matter how hard I tried, I would never be enough.

And this wasn't just any therapist. She had been present at my intake—one of the most soul-crushing experiences of my life. In that room, I'd been asked to recount, in minute detail, not only every trauma I'd endured but also every way I'd tried to cope. Every success. Every failure. Every crack in my foundation. I remember staring out the window as I spoke, wishing I were a bird that could fly away. She sat across from me as I bared it all, believing—hoping—it would be held with care. She knew what it had cost me to speak those things out loud. And still, she took what was meant to be confidential and used it as a punchline.

And she did it publicly—in front of other patients. It was cruel. It was inappropriate. It was a breach of trust. And it revealed something deeper about the culture I was in: a place that claimed to promote healing, but often punished people for trusting their own discernment. It wasn't just a moment of misjudgment. It was a reminder of how easily transparency can be twisted—how often people who've experienced trauma are expected to hand over their stories, only to have those stories used to reinforce the very shame they're trying to escape.

I could see it in her face; the regret hit the moment our eyes met. But the damage was already done. And the thing is, when you're already spiraling—physically depleted, emotionally exposed— moments like that can knock the wind out of you. Suddenly, every unfinished chapter in your life rushes back with claws. The dropped degrees. The jobs you left. The early exits. The times you walked away. In that fragile space, it's easy to wonder: Were they right about me?

But then I paused. And I remembered the truth. That I *did* use what I learned in the chiropractic program I left to become a highly effective anatomy and physiology professor for over a decade. That I *did* spend nine years teaching at one college. That I *did* earn a PhD and write multiple books. That I *did* build a business—one I've stayed with through all the uncertainty, all the pivots, all the starts and stops.

At the time, I didn't even have the energy to confront her. I was in such a dark place—fighting to be heard, struggling not to lose myself in the chaos of treatment—that her comment didn't even register as the worst thing that happened that week. But now, with distance and clarity, I can see just how wrong she was.

Yes, I've left things—not because I couldn't finish, but because they no longer aligned. Learning that was painful but powerful; it taught me to stop abandoning myself just to be seen as stable, good, or enough. Leaving isn't failure. Sometimes, walking away is its own form of completion—powerful in a way that staying never could be. But that kind of clarity comes at a cost.

Transparency doesn't guarantee care. Sometimes it makes you a target—labeled, misunderstood, pathologized. At times, it even brings punishment, especially in the very spaces that promised healing.

But the alternative? Staying silent? Smiling through someone else's version of my story while I quietly vanish inside myself? That's not safety. That's self-abandonment. And I've done enough of that to last a lifetime.

I learned that lesson early. I was twelve when one of my family members abused me. Some of my relatives knew, but a local attorney advised keeping quiet. It was a small town. There were family ties. There was shame. The message was clear: speaking up would only make things worse.

I remember feeling scared. Confused. Betrayed. Silenced. And not just by him, but by the people who were supposed to protect me. If the people I trusted most thought the best option was to keep quiet, what hope did I have of being heard anywhere else? So I held my tongue—not just about that, but about every other harm that came after. I learned to swallow my voice, to keep my pain hidden, to survive by disappearing. I decided that telling the truth didn't protect me; it just created more trouble.

Almost thirty years later, I found out that same man's daughter had accused him of the same kind of abuse. The news hit me like a punch. I couldn't help but wonder: if I had spoken up, could I have protected her? Could I have changed the trajectory of her life? I'll never know. I was only twelve. My family did what they thought was best with the knowledge they had. They thought they were protecting me.

But everything comes with a cost. Taking action and not taking action. Speaking up and staying silent. Taking risks and avoiding them. None of those paths are free. That's the lesson I carry now—not in a bitter way, but in a clear-eyed way. I see how the risks of staying silent, small, and comfortable can sometimes be far greater than the risks of stepping into the unknown.

That's why, as an adult, I take chances many people shy away from. I weigh the costs differently now, knowing that staying small and silent often carries greater risks than stepping into the places most won't dare to go. I won't let fear, shame, or someone else's comfort dictate the story I tell about my own life. Because the greatest cost I've ever paid wasn't from speaking up—it was from keeping quiet.

Being genuine hasn't always protected me from harm, but it *has* protected me from erasing myself. From going numb. From performing a version of myself that pleases everyone but starves my spirit. Telling the truth didn't erase the pain. But it made the pain worth something. It gave it a shape I could hold. It gave *me* a shape I could hold. And over time, it became less about being understood by everyone, and more about refusing to keep erasing myself for the comfort of others.

Radical transparency didn't save me from rejection. But it saved me from the quieter death of never being known. It's not that being real is always safe. It's that living unreal was quietly killing me.

But that doesn't mean it gets easier. In fact, the clearer you become, the more resistance you might meet. Don't expect applause for becoming who you are. Expect sideways comments. Expect guilt wrapped in concern. Expect silence where there used to be smiles. You might lose people—not always because they don't care, but because your clarity makes them question everything they're still hiding. Some will try to convince you that you've gone too far. Some will say they're worried. Some won't say anything at all—and the silence will sting more than their words ever could.

But don't let that confuse you. Their discomfort is not your danger. Every time you choose yourself—your voice, your energy, your truth—you're laying down a brick on the path of your becoming.

And yes, it's hard. But you're not weak for wanting peace and beauty and power in your own skin. You're not wrong for refusing to live ashamed.

So when the backlash comes, breathe. Ground. Return to your why. Remember: you're not doing this to be liked. You're doing this to be *free.*

And when they question you—gently or sharply, directly or indirectly—you don't owe them a defense. A simple, grounded truth will do. Something like: "I hear you. And I still choose this."

Because that's the thing about freedom: it's not about who agrees with you. It's about who you're willing to become, even when no one claps. And becoming yourself—fully, unapologetically—often means reclaiming the very traits you were once taught to shame.

So many of the things I once saw as flaws—my hyperindependence, my intensity, my high standards—were actually adaptations. They kept me alive. Focused. Functioning.

And yet, so many therapists tried to pathologize them. They read my drive as avoidance. They framed my leadership as overcompensation. They told me I needed to "slow down" or "do less"—not realizing that for me, movement was medicine. Purpose was anchoring. Expression was oxygen.

In many professional settings, especially for women or marginalized individuals, these same traits—drive, vision, intensity— are often reframed as liabilities. The workplace doesn't always know how to hold power that doesn't conform to comfort. And the same was true in therapy.

What they missed was this: I wasn't afraid to feel. I was afraid of drowning in feelings without a life raft. And now that I have one— now that I know how to come up for air—I can feel more safely. But I will never shame the version of me that moved fast. She was trying to outrun erasure. And she survived.

But survival doesn't come without residue. Even after the danger passes, the body remembers. The mind remembers. The old wiring doesn't disappear just because you finally feel safe. That's the thing about trauma—it lingers, not only in fear, but in how we relate to ourselves. In the way we brace, explain, overperform, apologize.

Shame, I've learned, is not an emotional flaw—it's a reflex. One I inherited from years of being watched, corrected, dismissed, and punished for simply existing. It didn't come out of nowhere. It was trained into me. Shaped by every sideways glance. Every sarcastic comment. Every time someone responded to my softness with scrutiny, or my truth with judgment.

Shame became my default interpretation. If someone crossed a line, I assumed it was because I let them. If someone withdrew, I assumed I pushed them. If someone disrespected me, I assumed I somehow deserved it. Even when I knew better logically, my body didn't believe it yet. Because shame doesn't live in the mind, it lives in the nervous system.

And over time, it fuses with your identity. It stops being something you feel and starts becoming who you think you are.

Especially when that shame gets reinforced by people who were supposed to protect you—or at the very least, not harm you. People like trusted adults. Former mentors. Past partners. Or even therapists.

That's what makes it so insidious. It doesn't just come from the people who outright hurt you. It comes from the ones who blurred the line between care and control. From the people who made you feel like their disappointment was your fault. From the ones who cloaked their manipulation in concern—or their predation in charm.

It's not just the trauma that lingers; it's the self-blame that follows. And when those patterns repeat across contexts—school, relationships, therapy, leadership—you start to wonder if maybe you *are* the common denominator. Maybe you are the problem. Maybe your voice really is too much. Maybe your needs really are unreasonable. Maybe your boundaries are just a cover for instability. Maybe you're reading into things. Making it up. Misunderstanding.

That's what shame does. It corrodes your clarity. It makes you question what your body knows. And the worst part? It doesn't need someone else to keep it going. Eventually, you start doing it to yourself.

You hear their voices in your own. You anticipate their judgments before anyone speaks. You police your truth. You put your healing on display. You shrink your power, just in case it threatens someone. Because somewhere along the way, your survival system got the message: being fully yourself is dangerous.

But here's what I'm learning: shame isn't a personality trait. It's a learned reflex—especially if you grew up in an environment where cruelty, criticism, or performance were normalized.

And the work now isn't to erase every trace of it. It's to recognize it when it shows up, and to meet it with something stronger. Something softer. Something that sounds like: "This isn't mine to carry anymore."

But just because I laid it down didn't mean others would. Letting go of inherited shame is hard enough—but what no one tells you is that shedding it publicly can invite a different kind of scrutiny. And even when I started doing the work—even when I named the patterns and took responsibility for the ways I'd protected myself through performance or control—I learned that honesty doesn't always earn you safety. In fact, sometimes the more honest you are about your shadows, the more others feel entitled to punish you for them.

Before entering treatment for my eating disorder, I wrote a list of things I needed to face. At the top was gossip. Not because someone else had called me out—but because I had. I knew it was a problem. I called it a "liability," because it was costing me trust, relationships, and credibility. I even wrote:

"I blame it on where I grew up, but I think it's really about getting attention—being noticed, having something interesting to say. My desire to be front and center… to not be invisible. But I've hurt people with this. I've lost credibility. And if I want to grow, I have to face it."

And I did. In group therapy for eating disorder treatment, I named it openly. I said that sometimes, when I didn't know how to connect, I'd gossip. That I had used other people's stories to feel significant. I didn't say it with pride. I said it because I was ready to stop performing.

But a few days later, during a meal break, some group members were talking about someone who had recently left the program. I wasn't saying anything. I wasn't even part of the conversation—just sitting at the table, eating quietly.

And then it happened. One of the group members who had been in the therapy session where I confessed that old habit turned to me, pointed her finger, and said: "You better not say anything about what you just heard."

It hit me like a punch. Not because she was wrong about gossip being harmful—but because she had taken something I vulnerably shared in a safe space and used it to shame me in public. I wasn't doing anything wrong. I hadn't even opened my mouth. But in her eyes, I was already guilty—because I had once named that tendency.

That moment taught me something I wish weren't true: Sometimes, the more honest you are about your shadows, the more others feel entitled to treat you like you're still living in them. And sometimes, even in spaces meant for healing, people will use your past as proof of your present—even when your actions don't match the accusation.

The same happens in organizational cultures that claim to value vulnerability, but quietly weaponize transparency when it threatens the hierarchy. This isn't just about personal betrayal; it's a cultural one.

It took time to unhook from that kind of shame. To remind myself that naming my patterns was an act of growth, not an invitation for public policing. And that transparency doesn't mean I owe everyone my trust. Honesty doesn't mean I forfeit my dignity.

That wasn't the only time I felt the consequences of being too transparent, too soon. There were jobs—leadership roles in higher education—where I watched trust erode not because of what I did recently, but because of stories I shared casually in the past. I thought I was building camaraderie. But sometimes, I was breaking confidence.

And I saw it in people's eyes—colleagues who once liked me pulling away. Students who stopped sharing. Conversations that shifted. Reputations that changed.

I kept thinking I could move cities, switch roles, start over. But every time I started over, I brought the same pattern with me—until I faced it. Until I owned it. Until I forgave myself.

I'm not proud of the ways I've broken trust. But I also won't let shame write my story. Because what started as a survival strategy—a way to feel noticed, powerful, central—is now something I can see clearly. And stop. And choose differently.

That's the work now. Not just being honest, but being whole. But wholeness isn't just about owning your impact. It's also about holding your boundaries. And sometimes, just when you think you've built a life around clarity and care, someone crosses a line that shatters the illusion of safety.

The violation from a trusted friend—the one I shared in Chapter 4, when I froze after he touched me without consent—happened on a Wednesday. Afterward, after the goodbye, the groan, the moment my body locked up, I got home and couldn't sit still. I didn't want to talk. I didn't want to think. I just wanted to erase it. Erase the feeling of his hands on me. Erase the sound he made. Erase the moment. Pretend it didn't happen. Pretend I was safe again.

I remembered that one of my neighbors—a friend who lived in my building—always went for drinks next door on Wednesday nights after work. I messaged him and asked if I could meet him there.

By the time I got to the bar, I could still feel the imprint of his hand on my right ass cheek. That's how vivid it was. That's how much my body still remembered. I scanned the room for the bartender and imagined what it would feel like to order a whole line of shots. One after another. Like I used to. Like I did in my twenties, when I didn't have the language for what I was carrying. When the only way I knew how to cope was to drink until I blacked out—until the ache turned to static and the night turned to nothing.

That part of me woke up again. She didn't want a drink. She wanted obliteration. She wanted to erase the moment, the ache, the memory—all of it. And I nearly gave in. But I didn't. Something in me held steady. Shaky, but steady. I sat at the bar, aching, unsettled—and I didn't drink. I talked to my friend. I told him I wasn't okay. I said just enough to not be alone with it. And that was enough to keep me from slipping back into the old way of surviving.

I didn't disappear that night. But I wanted to.

What scared me most wasn't the urge itself—it was how fast it came back. How easy it was to reach for an escape hatch I hadn't touched in years. I was 41. It was 2023. I hadn't been that girl for a long time. And yet she was right there, just beneath the surface, begging me to forget. Begging me to black it out.

And I'll be honest: part of what stopped me was fear—not just of what would happen that night, but of where it could lead. I know how easily one drink can become ten. I've seen it in my family. I've felt the addictive pull in my own body. And I've spent enough time crawling out of the dark to know I don't want to go back.

That moment—shaky as it was—was a kind of *embodied discernment*. I didn't need a script, a therapist, or a plan. My body knew. I knew. That version of escape wasn't safety. It was a detour back to the shame, the numbness, the self-erasure I've fought so hard to outgrow.

And even though it took everything in me to make a different choice, I did. I chose to stay with myself. To hold the ache instead of drowning it. To speak just enough truth to remain present. And that—quiet as it was—felt like power.

But the ache didn't end there. Because that's what betrayal does when it comes from someone who once felt safe—it scrambles your recovery. It calls into question your own discernment. It makes you want to turn off the part of you that trusted at all.

And this betrayal hit me on so many levels, because safety doesn't come easily for me. I've said before that solitude is my default. That even though I have a big personality—bubbly, animated, expressive— I feel most at ease when I'm by myself. I've shared that solitude is where I don't have to perform. But it's more than that. It's where I don't have to scan.

Because when I'm with people, I'm always scanning. If I'm not watching how I'm being perceived, I'm watching for signs of danger. My nervous system doesn't rest; it calculates. Constantly. Subtly. Desperately. I've lived through so many kinds of violation—verbal, physical, sexual—that being on guard became my baseline. I can feel it in my body every day: the tightness in my back, the tension in my jaw, the fractures in my teeth from clenching in my sleep. This is what hypervigilance does to a body over time.

So when I let someone in—especially a man—that's not small. That's not casual. That's years of dismantling my defenses just enough to exhale. That's years of proving to my nervous system that it's okay to trust *this one*. And he took that from me in a moment. He didn't just grope me. He detonated a safety I had worked years to build.

And in that moment at the bar, it wasn't just about drinking. It was about erasing all of it. Erasing the memory. Erasing the ache. Erasing *me*—the version of me that had started to believe it was safe to let someone in.

And still: I trust. Maybe that's the most radical part of all.

I've questioned whether I've revealed enough for this moment to land—whether I've shown you the depth of what it took to keep choosing love after so much loss. But the truth is, I don't need to share every wound. The ones I've named are enough. Enough to understand what it costs to stay open in a world that hasn't always met me gently.

Because if you've read what came before—if you've felt the weight of being misjudged, dismissed, touched without consent, written off, pathologized—then you know: the fact that I still let people close is nothing short of astonishing.

It amazes me, too. I could have easily ended up as a hermit on some remote island, walled off from the world. With all the heartache humans have caused me, you'd think I'd have given up on them by now. But I haven't. Somehow, I still have faith in people—maybe not blindly, but enough to keep showing up. Enough to keep letting others in.

That doesn't mean I move through life without protection. There are still moments when I carry the shell of a tortoise or the quills of a porcupine—instinctively guarding the softest parts of me. I know the exact second my body tenses, the instant my edges sharpen. But I've also learned these defenses aren't proof I've failed to heal. They're proof I've survived. They're the part of me that remembers—even when I wish it didn't—that trust is a risk. And I choose to take it anyway.

There were years when I didn't make that choice. Years when I let people just far enough in to feel connection, but not far enough to hurt me. I told myself I was protecting my peace—but what I was really doing was bracing for disappointment, keeping people at a distance I could safely recover from if they let me down.

And yet... I've softened. Not because I've stopped being afraid, but because I've gotten stronger. I can tell I've gotten stronger because I now let people closer than I ever have. I try again. I look for new therapists, even after the ones who failed me. I seek connection, even after the friendships that frayed. I still believe I could find a partner who meets me—fully, bravely—even after all the ones who didn't.

That belief isn't rooted in blind hope. It's guided by something deeper now—a kind of discernment I'm still learning to trust. After years of overriding my body through disordered eating and sleeping with men when what I longed for was safety, care, and belonging, it's not always easy to interpret what I feel. I still get confused. I still mistake activation for alignment. Sometimes my nervous system lights up not because I'm safe, but because I'm chasing the feeling of finally being chosen—fully, completely, without condition.

Not long ago, I told ChatGPT about this—about my fears that no man could love my body as it is, with its cellulite, scars, and history. I expected reassurance. What I didn't expect was a reframe that made my throat catch: "The man who is meant to love you will feel honored to touch a body that fought so hard to survive."

I had to pause before I could even repeat the word honored. It felt almost impossible—and yet, something in me knew it was the truth I'd been aching for all along. Not to be tolerated. Not to be loved in spite of. But to be cherished because of. That moment changed me. It shifted the question from "Will he accept me?" to "Who will meet my body with reverence?"

So now, I try to pause. To sit quietly. To listen beneath the hope. It takes practice. It takes patience. Especially when my body is flooded with excitement and my mind is busy writing the love story I've waited so long to live. But even in those moments, I'm learning to ask new questions—not "Will he choose me?" but "Do I feel safe choosing him?"

That shift—from proving my worth to honoring my knowing—is still unfolding. Some days, it's messy. Some days, I get it wrong. But I return to myself more quickly now. I hear the old ache and hold it with a new kind of tenderness. Because even when my body is unsure, my spirit remembers: I am allowed to choose, too.

That's one thing I'm most proud of. Not that I survived what happened. But that I didn't let it shut me down. That I still allow myself to love deeply. That I still let people in—not because I believe they won't hurt me, but because I believe I can handle it if they do.

Because the price of finding someone who sees me—someone who meets me with reverence and truth—is worth sifting through the ones who don't deserve to be that close. And I'm finally starting to trust myself enough to know the difference.

For years, I believed the problem was me. That if I had just been clearer, calmer, less emotional, maybe I wouldn't have been hurt so much. But now I know clarity doesn't always protect you from being used. Sometimes it just reveals who was never safe to begin with. Discernment, for me, is choosing how and where I am met—what I share, what I hold, and which rooms have earned access to my truth. That's the gift of discernment. It doesn't make the pain go away, but it ensures it's no longer mine to carry.

And maybe that's what I was really grieving all along. Not just the betrayals themselves—but the way I kept turning them inward, as if being misread was proof I had failed. It took me a long time to understand: being misunderstood doesn't mean you're broken. It doesn't mean you said too much or felt too deeply. Sometimes, it simply means someone wasn't ready—or willing—to see you clearly.

I've seen this play out not just in my personal life, but in professional spaces too—especially in environments where conformity is prized over candor.

Because I've always been hyperaware of how I'm being perceived—and willing to speak up in spaces where staying small is preferred—I've often had to absorb the weight of multiple colleagues and supervisors sending me the same message: *You're not okay as you are.* You're too much. You're not enough. You're unacceptable for one reason or another.

At one of the many institutions of higher education where I worked, I confided in my supervisor—a man I didn't fully trust—about how painful it was to know that so many people at the institution seemed to have a problem with me. I didn't feel safe with him, but I didn't know who else to turn to. Part of me still craved empathy. Or at least curiosity. Instead, he tilted his head and suggested, almost casually, that maybe I had a mental health issue. That maybe I should seek help.

He didn't consider for a second that I might be right; that my perception could be grounded in reality. That someone who overperforms, outshines others, and speaks her mind might, in fact, provoke discomfort. He didn't stop to think about the power dynamics at play, or how people sometimes respond to those they can't control. Instead, he labeled me as broken.

My heart sank. I tried not to let the shame take root—not to absorb yet another voice trying to convince me there was something wrong with me. But shame is a slippery thing. It knows the cracks in your history, the fault lines you've spent years trying to seal. And with a lifetime of battling this kind of messaging, it still found its way in.

And that's the pattern, isn't it? Different rooms, same script—clarity framed as threat, pride mistaken for instability.

For years, I carried moments like that as proof I was flawed. Now, I carry them as proof I showed up. That I told the truth. That I made myself visible in a world that prefers you palatable.

That's the shift. I no longer see being misread as a reason to shrink. I see it as a mirror—not a flawless one, but a revealing one. One that shows me where I've outgrown old roles. Where I'm no longer willing to edit myself for someone else's comfort.

And that's where we're headed next: not back into collapse, but into the clarity that comes when you stop performing and start witnessing yourself—not through someone else's lens, not through old roles, but with honesty and enough softness to stay whole.

What comes next isn't about being understood by everyone. It's about no longer abandoning yourself when you're not. It's about standing in front of the mirror—not to fix what's wrong, but to finally recognize what's always been real.

Still healing. Still becoming. But no longer vanishing to make others comfortable.

Because that's what discernment really is—not just knowing who to trust, but remembering I can trust myself. That's what all this integration has led me back to: the ability to feel my way through, to hear my own voice above the noise, to stand in front of the mirror and believe what I see. I may not have all the answers, but I've stopped looking for them in people who don't see me clearly. That alone is progress.

See Through Reflections

1. Personal Reflection

- Have you ever been punished for your pride, your clarity, or your self-awareness? What parts of yourself did you learn to hide in response?

- Which of your survival strategies have others misread as flaws—and what changes when you see them as proof of your strength?

- When have you felt most misunderstood—not because you were unclear, but because someone wasn't ready, or willing, to see you as you are?

2. Group or Cultural Exploration

- In your family, workplace, or culture, whose emotions are met with belief—and whose are questioned, dismissed, or pathologized?

- How do institutions (like education, healthcare, or religion) respond to people who express pride or power without apology? What does that reveal about what those systems protect?

- When someone is labeled instead of listened to, what ripple effects does that have—not just on them, but on everyone watching it happen?

3. Somatic/Embodied Practice

- Close your eyes and call to mind a moment when your joy, clarity, or confidence was misread as threat. Where does your body still hold that story? Place your hand there, if it feels safe. Whisper: "Your strength was never the danger."

- Let yourself move—even subtly—as if shaking off the weight of someone else's projection. Feel the difference in your body between shrinking for safety and standing in your full shape.

CHAPTER 7

Making Peace with the Mirror

It's 11:30 a.m. in Ho Chi Minh City. I'm sitting at my desk in nothing but underwear. The air conditioner hums weakly behind me—no match for the midday heat. I try not to look down. If I do, I'll see the sagging, the softness, the heat-slicked parts of me I've been trained to shame. My breasts. My belly. My thighs pressed wide against the chair.

This is not a triumphant moment, or a "made peace with the mirror" moment. This is a moment of holding—the kind I used to avoid by working, hiding, shrinking, fixing. Holding isn't passivity; it's how integration turns into power I can feel in my body. So today, I remain. I breathe. I write. I resist the urge to vanish.

Peace with the mirror, I'm learning, isn't a destination. It's not something you conquer. It's something you sit beside—gently, honestly—and choose not to run from. My healing didn't come from defeating the mirror. It came from being still in front of it. From sitting beside it and listening.

Because the mirror isn't just about my body. It reflects everything I've tried not to feel. The exhaustion. The ambition. The grief. The part of me that still wants to check out. It holds the weight of not being chosen, not being believed, not being enough—and the shame I've internalized just for existing in a body at all.

Making peace with the mirror means making peace with myself—with the hunger, the ache, the need, the softness, the rage. With the belief that being palatable is safer than being whole. And with the raw truth that sometimes being seen isn't glamorous or empowering. Sometimes it just feels like *emotional nudity*— standing still in the face of your own reflection, without armor or performance, and choosing to stay.

But the mirror isn't only on the wall. It's in your hand: a screen of curated images, comment threads, and dashboards pretending to measure your worth. I'm tired of waking up and letting an algorithm set my mood—whether followers tick up or down, whether a post 'lands,' whether anyone calls me inspiring that day. I'm not immune to the pull of praise or the sting of silence, and naming that is how I take the mic back. Naming separates truth from performance, self-trust from approval.

And that's why this chapter isn't a turning point—it's a continuation. Another layer of what I've been naming all along: the messiness, the tenderness, the truths that don't wrap up cleanly. Because being "see through" doesn't mean sharing everything. It means refusing to leave yourself, especially in the moments when slipping away would feel easier. It means staying honest when the shame creeps in. Letting the light in, even when it shows all the parts you're still learning to love.

And some of that truth lives in the body—the part of me that remembers things I haven't said out loud. The part that still braces, even when my mind knows I'm safe.

These days, when the old pain comes back—not in memory, but in sensation—I feel it in my chest. A tightening. A flutter of panic. Sometimes it builds. Sometimes it passes. But it's always familiar.

It usually shows up after I've revisited something raw. A memory. A story I haven't told in a while. The kind that doesn't just live in words, but in skin. I start to feel ungrounded. Agitated. My thoughts get faster. My body starts bracing. And part of me still wants to run to food.

When I'm in that state—tight-chested, tired, overstimulated—all I want is to leave the apartment, buy something indulgent, and eat until I don't feel anything. Ice cream. Chips. Bread. Sugar. Whatever might blur the sharpness. But lately, I've been trying something else first.

I lie down. Just for a short while. I don't hide under the covers or disappear for hours like I used to when I was depressed. Back then, I'd sleep the whole day away, then spiral harder for not getting anything done. Or I'd wake up at midnight with my sleep cycle broken and my mood worse.

Now I nap like a reset—twenty or thirty minutes, enough to let my system come back online and remind my body it's safe. Choosing a reset over a spiral is a quiet kind of power.

For years, I thought needing rest meant I was weak. That needing a nap after writing about trauma meant I was spiraling. But now I see those signals—the tightness in my chest, the ache in my neck—not as failures, but as invitations to slow down. There was a time I would've called this lazy. Or depressive. Or a setback. Now I know: it's just a reset.

Because I was conditioned to believe that fatigue, messiness, confusion, or slowness made me *less than*. That I had to be energized, clear, and competent at all times to be okay—let alone valuable. So when I felt foggy or flooded or slow, I panicked. I thought it meant I was broken again. Backsliding. Failing.

But the truth is: fatigue is human. So is sadness. So is the need to pause, soften, and start again. Now, when I lie down after an emotional surge, I don't shame myself for it. I see it as part of the process, part of being alive, part of being real. And it's in those moments of acceptance that I practice something new: noticing and choosing differently—again and again—until integration becomes power, not just language.

For years, I didn't just carry emotional weight—I carried physical weight, too. My weight has fluctuated more times than I can count. Right now, I'm overweight, and it's not because I've stopped trying or given up on myself. It's because I finally started recovering.

Six months ago, I entered eating disorder recovery. And one of the hardest parts hasn't been the behaviors—it's been the body image grief. The truth is, I'm still struggling to accept that weight gain is part of this process. That healing isn't always visible. That sometimes it looks like softness instead of strength.

I haven't finished mourning the image of perfection I chased for so long—the one I thought I needed to be lovable, respected, or enough. Somewhere deep down, there's still a belief that if I could just be thinner—or more toned, or more disciplined—maybe I'd finally feel worthy. But that belief has hurt me more than it's ever helped me. And I know it's time to let it go.

Still, I wonder: how do I accept a body I've spent a lifetime punishing? A body others have criticized, rejected, violated? A body I've hidden, starved, overworked, and shamed? How do I love a body that was never allowed to feel safe—not even with me?

I don't have a neat answer. But I do know this: my body is not the problem. The weight is not the problem. The problem was the world—

and my own conditioning—convincing me I was only valuable if I took up less space. That I had to disappear to be loved.

Now, I'm trying to unlearn that. To see my body not as a failure, but as a witness. A vessel that held every story I wasn't yet ready to tell. A journal written in curves and scars and stretch marks—not mistakes, but evidence. And maybe, over time, I'll learn to see that evidence not as shameful, but sacred.

When the tension rises and I feel that familiar pull, I don't always fight it—but I don't surrender blindly either. I pause. I let the quiet settle in just long enough to ask: *What am I really needing right now?*

Sometimes the answer is food. Sometimes it's not. But that pause—that moment of space between the trigger and the response—changes everything. Because for me, healing isn't about always getting it right. It's about offering myself the dignity of choosing with care. With awareness. With compassion.

That, too, is healing—not in how it looks, but in how it feels. Not in the absence of craving, but in the presence of choice.

That's a kind of power I never had before. Not because the panic is gone—but because I no longer confuse regulation with avoidance. I no longer need to numb to cope. And I don't shame myself when the impulse still shows up. I just meet it—gently, quietly—and begin again.

And that's what healing has become for me: not a perfect state, but a deeper knowing. A kind of clarity that says, *This feeling is familiar, but it's not a failure.* It's just part of the rhythm now—the ebb and return. The falling and the re-grounding. Not weakness. Not regression. Just being human—and letting that be enough.

I didn't always know how to sit still with myself. I first found that rhythm through movement—through climbing. Through the quiet truth-telling of a trail that demands your presence.

Before I ever sat still with a mirror, I climbed toward one. Mountains were where I first started to glimpse my strength—not just physically, but emotionally. Every summit was a mirror. Every sore muscle, a sentence in the journal my body was keeping long before I knew how to read it.

I didn't always know what I was healing when I climbed. I just knew that movement felt like medicine. That somewhere between the breathlessness and the views, I felt more whole. More honest. More me.

There was something about the mountain that didn't lie. It didn't care what I had accomplished, how I looked, or whether I believed in myself that day. It only reflected back what I brought to it: my grit, my grief, my persistence. And somehow, that was enough.

But healing wasn't linear on the trail, either. There were days I hiked strong and steady. Others where I collapsed in tears. My body— my knees, my back, my lungs—always let me know where I was pushing too hard. I just didn't always listen. Back then, I thought rest was weakness. Now I know: the body keeps score not to punish us, but to protect us. It's both compass and journal—keeping track of what needs tending and what needs to be released.

That's what I carried into this season, too. Even now—years later, continents away—I can feel the echoes of those mountains in me. They were where I first learned to stay with discomfort long enough to hear what it had to say.

Because what I'm learning is that some wounds don't just pass through; they anchor. Quietly. Deeply. Beneath the surface.

There's a plant called Japanese knotweed. It looks delicate above ground—soft leaves, gentle flowers. But its root system runs deep and wide. Left unchecked, it can destroy concrete foundations. That's how my trauma lived in me.

What showed up on the surface didn't look destructive. I looked fine—high-achieving, composed, strong. But underground, the roots were wrapping around everything: my sense of safety, my body image, my ability to rest—and the way I related to others. I didn't always see it clearly. And most of the world didn't either. I did my best to hide it, but the strain still leaked through—in my posture, in my pace, in how tightly I held myself together. The roots were there, quietly choking the foundation.

Healing, for me, has meant digging up what I couldn't always see. Not to rip it all out at once—but to name it, trace it, and meet the spaces it invaded. That's what integration looks like in practice—tending the roots, not just polishing the reflection.

But you can't trace the roots if you're always moving. You can't tend to what's buried if you're afraid to be still. And for most of my life, I was. Before I ever learned to sit with myself in stillness, I ran from silence. I filled every gap with noise, movement, work, food—anything to avoid the flood of thoughts waiting in the quiet. Stillness terrified me because I was convinced I'd unravel. I thought if I slowed down, everything I'd been holding back would come rushing in.

Yoga taught me a different rhythm. It trained me to sit with discomfort—and watch it pass. I began to see that not every difficult thought needed to be escaped. Some could be witnessed. Some could be softened. Some could even become doorways to healing.

In the beginning, I moved constantly—always on edge, always in motion. A boyfriend once said, "You bounce around like a jackrabbit," and he wasn't wrong. My nervous system was always bracing, always scanning, always trying to stay one step ahead of pain. Stillness used to feel like suffocation. But slowly, breath by breath, yoga changed that. It helped me trade chaos for clarity. Reactivity for response. Jackrabbit energy for grounded presence.

That's what yoga gave me: not just a more flexible body, but a more anchored life. A deeper ability to stay with myself, even when it was hard.

It also gave me the courage to look inward. For so long, I had been afraid of what I'd find. I thought my insides were too broken, too dark. But once I stopped running, I realized the truth: there was beauty in me, too. Creativity. Wisdom. Ideas I had never let myself explore because I was too busy trying to outrun the pain.

I've called my ego a life raft before—because that's what it was. It kept me afloat when the world told me I was nothing. But rafts aren't meant to be homes. They're meant to carry you to shore. For a long time, mine worked—a raft made of achievements, over-functioning, and self-inflation. But eventually, that ego began to morph into something else: a helium balloon, lifting me so high on praise and accomplishment that I started losing touch with the ground. I chased admiration instead of alignment. Performance instead of presence.

Yoga brought me back down. Not to deflate me, but to ground me. It gave me something I didn't know I needed: an identity that wasn't built on applause. A self that could exist without proving. A rhythm I could return to when the world—or my mind—got too loud.

And getting to where I could even begin that kind of work—where I could pause long enough to notice what lived beneath the surface— didn't happen by accident. It happened because I made space for it. Literally, emotionally, financially, spiritually. I didn't just stumble into healing. I built the conditions for it. I planned for it. I trusted myself to follow through on something I'd never done before.

That shift didn't happen overnight, but there was a moment when I knew I was ready. During the final months of my last full-time job, something in me began to change. Not in a fleeting way, but in a foundational one. I could feel the buildup of everything I had been circling finally rising to the surface. I was exhausted, yes—but not just from overworking. I was exhausted from avoiding what I knew I needed most: stillness, space, and the chance to stop performing long enough to take care of myself.

I had spent over 30 years with an eating disorder, and just as many years working. I started earning money when I was twelve and never stopped. Babysitting. Teaching. Coaching. Writing. Speaking. Leading. Building. Always running on adrenaline. Holding together image and survival and grit and goals. For most of my adult life, I wasn't just working full-time—I was working multiple jobs: managing a business, teaching part-time, publishing books, volunteering, traveling, hiking mountains. Always going. Always achieving. Always managing the next thing. I only stopped working full-time six months ago, and it's the first time in my life I've had space to truly slow down.

And in many ways, that movement was protective. It kept me from sitting in the ache of what I hadn't yet faced. If I just kept moving, maybe my past couldn't catch up to me. Maybe I wouldn't have to feel what it meant to be told, as a little girl, that I was nothing. That I would never be anything. That I didn't matter.

But the past doesn't disappear just because you outrun it. It waits. It waits until you're quiet enough to hear what it's been trying to say all along.

I knew—I *knew*— that if I wanted to truly heal, I couldn't keep doing it in the background of someone else's demands. I couldn't fully take care of myself while working for institutions that drained me. I couldn't keep holding space for everyone else while ignoring the child in me who never got the space she needed.

So I made a plan. I started saving years before I was ready to leap. I built a financial runway not because I was ready to use it, but because I believed that one day I would be. I didn't know exactly when, but I knew that when the time came, I wanted to be able to walk away from everything that was no longer aligned—and have the freedom to finally sit with myself. And that's exactly what I did.

But it wasn't just about leaving a job. It was about walking away from a kind of life that required constant maintenance. These days, all my belongings fit in a few bags. I don't have a kitchen to clean, a closet to organize, or bills to juggle in the ways I used to. And that's not because I've escaped responsibility—it's because I've stripped my life down to what matters. Even though I'm gallivanting around the world, my lifestyle is simpler now than it's ever been. I stay in places where someone else does the cleaning. Where I don't have to think about cable bills, car repairs, or coordinating ten different obligations. My decisions are quieter now: Am I going to rest today? Am I going to write? Do I need to slow down or keep moving? And more often than not, the answer is within reach—because I've created a life that gives me that choice.

This simplicity wasn't a coincidence. It was intentional. I let go of what wasn't aligned—not just the obvious obligations, but the hidden clutter, the emotional noise, the background pressure that kept me performing strength long after I was spent. And in letting go of all that, I gained something I didn't even know I was missing: space to actually feel. To recalibrate. To ask what I needed—and then give it to myself, without a dozen other things pulling at me.

To be clear, none of this was impulsive or careless. It was sacred. I left my last job. I gave away thousands of dollars of belongings. I let go of everything I didn't want to carry into the next chapter. Not just furniture and clothes—but identities, obligations, relationships, habits. I shed my life. And with every layer I released, something else opened up. My nervous system started to settle. My voice got clearer. My patterns got quieter. The things I used to tolerate suddenly felt intolerable.

But that doesn't mean it was easy. These last six months—the first stretch of time where my only job has been to care for myself and build what I truly believe in—have brought more spiritual resistance than I ever could have anticipated. It's like the universe heard me say, "I'm ready to let go of these limiting beliefs," and immediately said, "Prove it." People showed up to test my boundaries. Institutions pushed back. The eating disorder recovery clinic I entered with such hope turned out to be a battleground of projection and dismissal. Men entered my life and disrupted it. Old stories tried to pull me back.

But I didn't abandon myself. Not this time. Because here's what I've learned: power doesn't always look like forward momentum. Sometimes, it looks like *staying put.* Sitting in the discomfort instead of escaping it. Holding space for fear without feeding it. Reminding yourself, even when doubt creeps in, *I planned for this. I prepared for this. I chose this.*

And I'm proud of that. I'm proud that I trusted myself enough to stop. I'm proud that I saved—not just money, but energy. Faith. Courage. I'm proud that I created the space I once thought was impossible. And I'm proud that I've used that space not just to rest, but to *become.* Not the version of me I thought the world wanted. But the one I've been slowly, gently, finally becoming.

This wasn't just a career change. This was a soul-level shift. And no matter what comes next, I know I'll look back on this season as the one where I chose myself—fully, without apology—for the very first time.

But I'll be honest—part of me hesitates to even say all of this. To say out loud that I saved enough money to walk away from my job. That I created space to rest. That I gave myself time. Because I know what some people will think. I've heard it before—in passing comments, in book reviews, in thinly veiled judgments. *Must be nice. You're so lucky. Some of us don't have that option.*

That word *lucky* hits a nerve every time. Yes, I've had privileges I won't deny. I was born in America. I'm white. I have people in my life who love me. I've had moments of access and support that others haven't. But I also wasn't handed this life. I built it—methodically, intentionally, over time. That's power to me: designing the conditions where healing can actually happen.

In fact, I started building *this* chapter of my life—the one rooted in freedom, full-time travel, and living on my own terms—back in 2018. It remains one of the best years of my life, marked by adventures across five continents. I hiked through the wilderness of Tanzania, summited Mount Kilimanjaro—the highest point in Africa—and later, Mount Elbrus, the highest in Europe. I spent 33 days traveling east to west through Russia, my soul stretching wider with every mile. I flew like a bird through the sky while paragliding, the wind on my face a kind of freedom I'd never known. And as a biology professor, nothing delighted me more than walking in Darwin's footsteps through Chile's La Campana National Park, tracing biodiversity with a local biologist in the Chilean palm forest.

That year wasn't just about adventure; it was about clarity. Something clicked in me. I realized I didn't want these kinds of experiences to be rare. I wanted them to be the *norm*. I didn't want someone else deciding when I could travel, how long I could go, or how much time I could take off before I was punished with judgment or financial strain. I wanted freedom. I wanted time. I wanted wealth—not just to accumulate money, but to have options. I wanted to live a life where my days were mine. And I wanted to do it while helping others rise from difficulty, too.

So I made a commitment—and then built my life around it. I imagined the exact life I wanted, then worked backward. I asked: *What would it take to create this kind of freedom? What skills do I already have? What kind of work would feel meaningful—but not require going back to school for another degree?* I already had twelve years of higher education under my belt and nearly $200,000 in student loan debt. I'd finished my PhD just six years earlier—and I needed a break. I wasn't opposed to more formal education someday, but at that point, I couldn't justify the time, energy, or financial strain of another degree. So I chose a different path. One where I could build on what I already knew—not just academically, but experientially. One where I could keep learning through targeted certifications and practical tools, while also making a difference through the wisdom I'd earned by living it. That's when I discovered life coaching. It was a path where I could use my story, my resilience, my training, and my heart—and do it on my own terms.

That same year—2018—I started my business: *Serotinous Life*. A name rooted in biology, because life—and the study of it—had always been at the core of my work. But it went deeper than that. The concept of *serotiny* refers to seeds that only release in response to an environmental trigger—often fire. And that's what trauma had been for me: fire. Destructive, yes. But also the thing that cracked me open and made my growth possible.

Serotinous cones don't open when it's safe or merely because it's time; they open because of fire. The heat is what forces the cone to release its seeds. Without that trigger, they stay sealed. And that's how I see my own story: I don't think I'd have this level of drive, or this deep hunger for life, if it weren't for my own fires. My trauma didn't just shape me—it activated something in me that might have otherwise stayed dormant.

And that's what I wanted my coaching practice to reflect—not just surviving trauma, but growing *because* of it. That idea—that adversity can spark transformation—is the foundation of something called *post-traumatic growth*. It doesn't justify harm; it names what I made from it. It's still a relatively new concept for many people, but it's the heart of my work: helping others recognize that the fire didn't destroy them—it revealed what was waiting to grow.

But just because I had the vision didn't mean the path was easy. The truth is, it's astonishing that I'm not a drug addict, or in an abusive relationship, or living a life completely consumed by dysfunction—not because I'm better than anyone who is, but because the odds were stacked against me, too. I wasn't supposed to make it here. People tried to bury me. They pushed my face into the dirt. And I kept getting back up.

What so many people don't see—and maybe don't want to see—is that this life wasn't given to me. It wasn't luck. It was built on years of invisible decisions. I wore used clothes. Drove the same car for over a decade. Lived below my means. I chose simplicity—not because it was easy, but because it created room for what I was working toward.

I did all of this while holding down multiple roles: full-time job, business owner, writer, teacher, hiker, volunteer—constantly performing strength while unraveling privately. None of it was glamorous. None of it was easy. But I did it because I *knew* I'd need space one day to finally heal. And I wanted to be ready.

But it didn't just take seven years to get here—it took a lifetime. This moment—writing these words from Asia, living in the freedom I once only imagined—may have been seven years in the making, but those years were built on everything that came before: the early abuse, the sudden death of my partner at twenty-five, the years of suicidal thoughts and survival-mode living. I didn't just wake up one day and start designing a better life. I had to claw my way toward the belief that a better life was even possible.

And once I caught a glimpse of it—once I stopped living from a place of constant reaction—I devoted myself to something else entirely: creation.

For most of my healing journey, I fit the definition of *performance-based recovery*. By that I mean recovery that looked impressive from the outside: milestones stacked, credentials earned, the right language spoken—all while my nervous system still white-knuckled its way through. I wanted to be seen as strong, self-aware, resilient, even when I was unraveling inside. I didn't know it at the time, but I wasn't just healing; I was staging it, trying to stay one step ahead of shame.

Even writing this book tempts me to fall back into that pattern—to wrap everything in a bow, to avoid admitting how often I still backslide. But I've lived through an incredibly complex set of experiences. Of course the healing would be complex too. How could it not be?

Only recently have I embraced *self-designed healing*: a path that prioritizes honesty over performance, and presence over perfection. It's not linear. It rarely looks impressive. And it almost never feels comfortable. But it's grounded in truth. It's not about fixing what's "wrong" with me—it's about listening to what's real. About honoring what I need, even when no one else is watching.

And that's the path I want to keep choosing. Not the performance; the presence. Not the illusion of being done, but the reality of still becoming.

This journey hasn't been easy. But I've never felt more proud. Because I trusted myself. Because I sold what I needed to sell. Because I made the leap—and caught myself. And even when things were hard—with the elephants, with rejection, with volunteering—I never once wished I had stayed behind. I've said it to every friend and family member I've talked to along the way: this was the best decision I could've made. Not because it's been smooth, but because it's been aligned with who I really am.

I didn't just quit my job and take off. I planned. I tested. I asked hard questions—What's working? What's not? Where am I shrinking?

What needs to change?—and kept adjusting until my life aligned with what I envisioned. This wasn't about a single breakthrough. It was a thousand tiny decisions over decades—and I kept choosing forward.

There were so many easier options. I could've stayed in jobs that burned me out. I could've kept running from the deeper work. I could've stayed quiet when I witnessed harm. Let the old patterns keep me small. And yes—there were moments when giving up felt easier, too. When the weight of what I carried made me question whether it was worth continuing at all.

But I didn't stop. I chose the harder path, again and again. I chose to speak up, even when my voice shook. To rest, even when I feared judgment. To sit with the discomfort of my story instead of avoiding it for another decade. I chose to believe in a future no one could hand me—one I had to build for myself.

So no, I'm not here because I'm lucky. I'm here because I did the work. I made unseen sacrifices and showed up when it was terrifying. I stayed with myself when it would've been easier to walk away. I'm here because I stopped letting other people define my worth—and because I finally got tired of shrinking to make others more comfortable.

And still, I know there will be people who dismiss me anyway. Who assume I had it easier than I did. Who try to discredit what I've built by chalking it up to privilege or coincidence. Who try to put me back into a box that feels easier to explain. But even then—I keep going. Because I'm done apologizing for being here. I'm done explaining away what I've earned. I'm done trying to prove that I deserve a seat at the table. I do. And I'm not giving it up.

But after moments like that—moments when I refuse to shrink, when I take up space without apology—I almost always feel the ripple. The energetic comedown. The need to return to myself and recalibrate. Because staying visible isn't just about speaking truth. It's about tending to what that truth stirs up inside me. The fear. The fatigue. The ache of being seen.

After volunteering at the elephant sanctuary in Thailand, I spent a week and a half in Chiang Mai. I stayed in a small condo just outside the city—a quiet space where I could swim, rest, and work on my business. It rained most days. Not a soft drizzle, but a steady, soaking rain that seeped into my shoes, clung to my clothes, and eventually crept into my mood. Still, I tried to stay present. To let it be what it was.

Midway through my stay, I signed up for a full-day countryside tour. We drove through winding hills and stopped at a few scenic spots along the way, most of them gentle and accessible. But by mid-afternoon, we reached a trailhead for a steep hike—and that's when my back started screaming. I gave it thirty minutes. Tried to keep up. But the pain was too sharp, and I knew if I pushed through it, I'd pay for it later. So I turned around. I told the group I was heading back and made the descent alone. I knew it was the right decision. And it still stung.

That old shame came flooding back—the one that says, *You're falling behind. You're weak. You're not enough.* I hated how quickly those thoughts surfaced. I hated how much I still believed that slowness meant failure. I hated that this body, the one I had worked so hard to love, couldn't keep up the way it used to.

That ache stayed with me as the day unfolded. The kind of ache that has less to do with pain and more to do with the grief of who you used to be. I was in a beautiful place, and I couldn't fully reach it.

But then—just before sunset, at our final stop—something shifted. We pulled up to the last site of the day: a roaring waterfall surrounded by thick green forest. And for the first time that day, the rain stopped. The clouds began to lift. The air was still damp, but no longer heavy. My limbs still ached, but something in me softened.

We walked along a paved trail, following the sound of rushing water. It grew louder with every step—insistent, alive. And then there it was: a towering cascade, thundering over rock. Water spraying in every direction. Unapologetic. Wild. Beautiful.

The closer we got, the wetter we became—not from rain, but from the mist shooting out from the base of the falls. It clung to my arms, my face, my clothes. And I didn't flinch. I didn't shield myself. I let it land. I came alive.

There was something about that moment—the sun finally breaking through, the spray on my skin, the roar in my ears—that cracked something open in me. The weight I had been carrying, both physically and emotionally, started to lift. Not all of it. Not forever. But enough to remember who I was beneath the ache.

For a moment, I felt as if the rain in Thailand had washed my pain away. When the fog cleared, I could see me—all of me—my parts integrated into one beautiful being who's a mixture of strength, silliness, independence, and sass operating in unison.

Not the version who turned back on the hike. Not the one who felt ashamed or behind. But the one who stayed. The one who didn't abandon herself when it hurt. The one who let the day be imperfect and chose to show up anyway.

That version of me—the one who laughed in the mist, who didn't care that she looked like a drowned kitten, who walked barefoot across the slick stone path just to see the waterfall from every angle— she wasn't new. She had always been there. But that day, she wasn't hiding.

Yes, other people were there. Some looked at me like I was a little crazy—walking around barefoot, hair soaked, grinning like a kid— but I didn't care. I've always loved feeling my feet on the earth. I grew up in the Adirondacks. I used to teach barefoot. It's how I remember I'm still here. Still alive.

And that's how I felt in that moment: alive. Not in spite of my body, but because I stayed with it. I let it ache. I didn't rush to escape or override the disappointment. I chose presence over perfection.

That choice might sound simple, but for me it wasn't. I've spent most of my life running from pain, either by pushing it away or powering through it. Staying is new. It's something I once practiced on the yoga mat—through stillness, through breath—but somewhere along the way, I lost touch with it. I forgot what it meant to remain. Why it mattered. And why it's called a practice: not something you master, something you return to. Like the mountain trail. Like the nap after a flood of emotion. Like the air that steadies you when everything else feels out of reach.

I used to think healing was a before-and-after photo, something you could measure in progress pictures or milestones. I used to believe it meant the end of struggle. But the mirror still wavers. Some days, my body feels like a warzone; other days, a sanctuary. The difference isn't in how I look; it's in how I show up. How I stay. How I tend to the roots without running. How I keep meeting myself, even in the fog.

That moment at the waterfall didn't fix everything, but it anchored something—a truth I'd been chasing in a thousand ways that finally landed without effort: I don't have to be healed to feel joy. Travel helped me practice this work, but it isn't required. The real work is local and daily: boundaries, self-trust, and telling the truth where you already live. I just have to remain, in my body, with my breath, with myself.

I had been practicing staying with myself—through discomfort, through longing, through the moments that used to send me spiraling. But there's a different kind of healing that happens when someone else sees you… and chooses to remain, too.

There's something healing about being seen in your softness—not just when you're soaring, but when you're struggling. And for a long time, I didn't believe that kind of love was available to me. Especially not from men.

Most of my trauma involved being hurt by people—many of them men—who saw me as an object, not a person. So I learned early on that being wanted didn't mean being cared for. That attention wasn't the same thing as affection. And that love—if it existed at all—came with conditions. Sex. Compliance. Smiling through pain.

It's no wonder that, for most of my life, I kept people at arm's length. Or that I mistook control for connection. Even as I healed, that belief—that I was only lovable if I was pleasing—was hard to shake. Then came Chris.

We met years into my healing journey. He's married, grounded, and kind. There's never been a single moment of sexual tension between us. And maybe that's part of why his presence feels so safe. So steady. So... unfamiliar.

There's no ambiguity. No undertone. Just friendship. Just care. His loyalty to his wife has always been clear, and his integrity is unwavering—which somehow makes his love feel even safer. It shows me that connection doesn't have to be complicated to be real.

I'm not used to being loved by a man who expects nothing in return. Not my body. Not my emotional labor. Not my performance. Just me.

Our friendship became one of the most important mirrors in my life—the kind that didn't distort or demand. One day, during a walk, I admitted I'd been struggling. I was raw. Foggy. Not my best self. And I almost canceled because of it. I didn't want him to see me like that— sad, vulnerable, unpolished. A part of me still believed that showing my pain would scare people away.

But he stayed right there—steady, kind, unchanged. He listened. He cared. He held space. And before we said goodbye, he looked me in the eye and said, "I love you." Not as an act. Not to get something. Not out of obligation. He said it because he meant it.

And I let it in. Not all at once. Not without discomfort. But I let it land—not just in my mind, but in my body. It was awkward at first, being loved like that. But it was also profound. Because it wasn't just about him—it was about me. About the version of me that finally felt safe enough to stay. To be loved without needing to earn it.

That kind of safety was new. And fragile. But it was real—not because it was constant, but because I could finally feel it. I didn't have to perform for it. I didn't have to prove anything. I just had to let it in.

Chris didn't heal all the old wounds. But he helped me rewrite one of the oldest lies—that love is conditional, and I'm only worthy of it when I'm perfect. His love didn't ask me to change. It didn't retreat when I was messy. It stayed. And that gave me the courage to stay, too—not just in friendship, but in myself.

That moment, like the waterfall, anchored something. A truth I'd always longed to believe: I don't have to prove my worth to be loved. I just have to keep showing up as myself.

But it's strange how quickly power can shift. Just twelve hours before the encounter with that man on Monkey Island—the one who called me a victim and made me shrink—I was anything but small.

At 11:15 p.m. the night before the tour, someone tried to open my door. I was in bed, unclothed, trying to fall asleep before my early wake-up. At first, they knocked. Then the doorknob started rattling. Then came the sound of keys—someone trying to unlock it. I jolted upright, shoulders up around my ears, my nervous system instantly on high alert. I shouted, "Wait!" But the jiggling didn't stop. I rushed to throw on clothes. My heart was pounding. My brain was cycling through worst-case scenarios—because for someone with a history like mine, this wasn't just startling. It was terrifying.

I yelled louder this time. "Fucking wait!" And when I flung the door open—ready for a fight—I didn't shrink.

I didn't care that it was a group of uniformed officers. I didn't care that the building owner stood there too. I stood in the doorway—firm, unshaken—and asked, "What is going on?" At first, they just said they needed to see the passports of all foreigners in the building. No explanation. No courtesy. Just a demand. I handed over my documents, but I didn't do it quietly. I kept asking questions—pressing for clarity. That's when the truth came out: they were checking for drugs. The owner, who had seemed neutral at first, shifted. When I didn't comply passively, when I dared to question what was happening, he rolled his eyes—irritated that I was making noise instead of just playing along.

Eventually, the police returned my documents. I asked, "Can I go back to bed now?" The officer said yes. But of course, I couldn't sleep. I lay awake for hours—too rattled to rest—and when I finally dozed off, there were only three hours left before I had to wake up for the tour.

So when I got to Monkey Island that morning, I was already frayed. Sleep-deprived. Tender. Tired in every way. And that's part of what made what happened next so hard. Because that same woman who had stood tall in front of four men at midnight—three of them police officers—completely caved under the words of one older American man.

He wasn't threatening. He wasn't yelling. We'd actually been chatting for ten minutes before the monkeys came. I had let my guard down. He seemed harmless. Safe. But the moment I screamed in fear—instinctive, primal—something shifted. He turned on me.

Shamed me. Made me feel like I was crazy for reacting to a monkey attack. And I shrank.

What happened wasn't just about him—it was what some therapists call an *emotional flashback*. A surge of shame and fear that felt bigger than the moment because it carried the weight of every moment like it.

That's what stung the most. Not just what he said, but the way I crumpled under it. After everything I've lived through. After all the progress I've made. It wasn't logic that collapsed. It was muscle memory. The old pattern of cowering when someone poked a wound I thought had healed.

But I can see the difference now. That collapse? It wasn't weakness. It was fatigue. It was humanity. The night before, I had to be fierce just to protect my body. The next day, I didn't expect to need armor. And that's the cost of surviving in a world that can turn on you at any moment—you never know when to brace.

Still, something's changed. I didn't stay collapsed. I didn't spiral for days. I reflected. I rewrote. I reclaimed. And that's what power looks like now—not perfection, but recovery. The ability to come back to myself. To say, "Yes, I shrank. And then I stood up again."

Before the police incident and Monkey Island—and just after I left a physically and emotionally draining volunteer experience in northern Vietnam—I walked into a recording studio in Ho Chi Minh City to begin work on the audiobook for my third book, *Moving Forward*. It was July 3rd. I was exhausted. Tender. Still coming down from everything I had held together at that school. But I had a job to do, and I didn't want my emotions to interfere.

I'd recorded audiobooks before, but never in a space like this— never with someone I didn't know at all. The studio engineer was polite, respectful, and professional. But my nervous system didn't care. It read the unfamiliarity as risk.

Immediately, I found myself slipping into old patterns—scanning for signs of disapproval, trying to anticipate judgment. I was overly focused on how he might be perceiving me. Was I speaking too fast? Too slow? Too flat? Too emotional? I kept editing myself mid-sentence, worrying that every imperfection would make me look unqualified—like I didn't belong behind the mic.

He hadn't done anything to make me feel that way. But the shame still surged. It was the same old voice on loop: *You must be perfect to be good enough. If you mess this up, you'll be exposed.*

In the past, I would've hidden that. Smiled through the panic. This time I tried something different. I said, "I'm feeling a little off today. It isn't about you; I'm just in my head." Naming it out loud wasn't an accident. It was a skill I'd fought hard to learn.

That simple act of speaking it shifted something. The tension didn't vanish, but it softened. I didn't feel like I had to pretend, and that made all the difference.

Over the next three sessions, everything started to feel lighter. My voice steadied. My pace improved. The fear of being judged was still there, but it didn't control me anymore. With each recording day, I got more comfortable—not just with the engineer, but with myself. Because I wasn't hiding. I wasn't overcorrecting or compensating. I was just showing up.

And that's what growth has started to look like for me: not perfection, but presence. Not eliminating fear, but meeting it with truth. I'm not beyond the reach of insecurity—especially in unfamiliar or evaluative spaces—but I'm no longer ruled by it.

That recording wasn't just about narrating a book. It was about living it. Moving forward, not because everything is fixed—but because I trust myself to keep going, even when my voice shakes.

Before heading back into the recording studio, I treated myself to a massage at the same spa where I'd recently gotten my cosmetic tattooing—a space that had already held pieces of my healing. The spa was serene and luxurious—a small sanctuary tucked into the noise of Ho Chi Minh City—and I knew my body needed that care. Recording *Moving Forward* was already pushing me to revisit old pain with new presence, and even though the words were scripted, the emotions they stirred were not. During that last recording session, I had needed to step away a few times—not because I couldn't handle it, but because I was learning to honor the moments when my nervous system needed space. Tears never fully spilled, but they welled. My throat tightened. My chest ached. And instead of pushing through like I used to, I let myself pause.

That morning, I chose massage not as a reward, but as a reset. A way to ground myself before going back into the recording booth and reading out loud the very stories that had once made me want to disappear.

Massage has long been part of my healing. I wrote about it in my first book, *Transformation After Trauma*— how safe, intentional human touch helped me begin to reclaim my body as worthy. That realization wasn't new. But what happened that morning reminded me how important it still is. This time, tears didn't well. Instead, I started to smile. Because I honored what I needed.

When the pressure was too firm, I spoke up. When a position strained my lower back, I asked for an adjustment. And I didn't feel bad about it. I didn't silence myself to make someone else more comfortable. I didn't override my own body's needs to avoid seeming high-maintenance or hard to please.

That may not sound revolutionary, but for me it was. Not because I discovered something new, but because I chose to live what I already knew: asking for what I need isn't a burden. It's a self-honoring act. It's not about being difficult—it's about being honest. And that morning, honesty felt like kindness.

It reminded me that I don't need a partner to receive nurturing, healing touch. I haven't been in a long-term relationship in years, and while I miss the physical closeness, this massage reminded me that I don't have to wait for the right man to come along to experience the benefits of being held or cared for. I don't have to carry the pressure of wondering whether my body is desirable enough or okay enough for someone else. A massage, at its best, isn't about being judged—it's about being supported. It's about taking care of me. And when the touch is safe, skilled, and respectful, even in a professional setting, it can offer something sacred: the chance to feel comfort in my body without conditions.

That kind of comfort once felt unreachable to me—unless it came from being desired. For a long time, I believed the only way to feel okay in my body was through someone else's attraction.

There was a time when being wanted felt like the highest form of validation I could receive. If a man with a sculpted, conventionally attractive body wanted to touch mine, then surely my body couldn't be that bad. That's the story I used to cling to. The logic I used to soothe the ache—as if someone else's desire could override the years of shame I carried. As if their attention could undo the hurtful words I'd absorbed about my body from the world, and from myself.

But that logic was born from distortion—from a lifetime of being treated like an object, not a person. I was praised when I looked small and punished when I didn't. I learned early that desire didn't always mean care. That being wanted wasn't the same as being valued. And that if someone loved me, it was often because of how well I played the part—not how fully I let myself be seen.

I've worked too hard to unlearn all that. Too hard to come home to a body I once starved, punished, and tried to disappear. These days, when someone casually remarks that women who are "fit" are more attractive—or implies that physical culture is a requirement for love—

I pause. I let my nervous system speak before I let the old craving to be chosen take over. Because I've realized something essential: if being loved means hating myself again, it's not love.

I used to believe I had to betray my body in order to be touched—to shrink, to play the role, to tolerate discomfort just to feel wanted. But not anymore. There is no version of healing where I abandon myself to be held.

I've worked too hard to reclaim my softness as sacred—to see my stretch marks not as shame, but as story. So I'm learning to remain loyal to the truth I've earned: that I am lovable in this body, now. That worth isn't something I have to diet or hustle my way into. And that the strongest thing I can do is stay; not shrink.

I used to think I needed to be chosen to feel valuable—that someone else's desire could prove my worth. But I don't want that kind of proof anymore. I want peace. And peace doesn't come from disappearing. In fact, if being desired demands I erase myself, it's not desire—it's danger.

We live in a culture that confuses desirability with value, praising women for shrinking and quieting themselves to fit a fantasy. But that's not love. That's control. And I'm no longer interested in shaping myself for systems that reward my silence.

So I'm choosing something different now. I'm choosing to remain with the body I have, with the truth I've claimed, with the version of me that no longer needs to earn love by erasing herself. Because that's where my power lives—not in being chosen, but in refusing to abandon myself to be.

And maybe that's why it strikes me when people worry I'll forget them. I've spent so much of my own life doing the opposite—making sure I couldn't be forgotten.

It's interesting to me how often people have said, "I don't know if you remember me"—or told me not to forget them. That's rarely a fear

I carry. I spent my childhood feeling invisible, but I've spent most of my adulthood making myself unforgettable. Performer. Storyteller. Captivating. For men, sexy. For the world, unique. Intriguing. I built a presence no one could easily erase—partly from ego, partly from survival, and partly because I was tired of being forced behind a locked door and only let out when someone else decided I was allowed to be seen.

And I love that I'm unforgettable now—not because I want others to feel small, but because I've stopped making myself small. Stopped hiding. Stopped pretending I could only take up space if it was convenient for someone else.

Still, staying visible isn't the same as being immune to the old narratives. The voices that taught me to shrink haven't vanished. Sometimes Diablo shows up with the same ferocity he always had—making me flinch at stretch marks, wince at softness, recoil from the mirror like I did when I was twelve. Some days, I still hear the shame loud and clear. But I don't obey it like I used to. I don't make it gospel. I just keep returning—to the beliefs I'm building, to the body I'm learning to stay with, to the life I want now. Over and over, I return to myself.

And sometimes, coming back to myself means laughing in the middle of a scene I couldn't have scripted—the kind that reminds me I don't need to control every moment to own it. A few weeks after Japan—where I'd face-planted in a crowded walkway and flashed my modest underwear to half of Tokyo—Vietnam gave me the sequel I didn't know I needed.

I'd arrived in Hanoi late at night from Thailand, dragging three pieces of luggage and wearing the same black dress from my Japanese wipeout. My Grab driver couldn't get down the narrow lanes to my guesthouse—roads so tight they were more suggestion than street, meant for motorbikes, not cars. He called the guesthouse, and a young man appeared on a motorbike, gesturing for me to hop on.

There were two small problems. First, I'd never been on a motorbike in my life. Second, I was traveling with three bags and wearing a dress that was absolutely not designed for mounting a bike in the traditional way—straddling the seat with one leg swung over. I had no idea how to do that without flashing the entire crowd of strangers that had gathered to watch this scene unfold.

Somehow, he wedged my midsize suitcase between his legs, I strapped my small backpack to my front, my larger backpack to my back, and perched side-saddle, gripping him awkwardly. Before we even pulled away, I blurted, "I don't even know who you are."

"That's okay," he grinned. "I know who you are."

We took off—and by "took off," I mean lurched into a sharp turn. Between the backpack imbalance, my inexperience, and the side-saddle position, I promptly tipped backward. In Japan, I'd fallen forward. In Vietnam, I fell back. In both countries, my dress flew up in front of a ring of strangers. At least I'd chosen modest underwear both times.

This time, though, I laughed. Hard. Maybe because I wasn't rushing for a flight. Maybe because I wasn't scraped and bruised. Or maybe because the gap between the two falls—just a few weeks—had shown me how much more quickly I could recover now.

When we finally arrived, the young man asked my age. I told him I was forty-three. His eyes widened. "I thought you were in your early thirties. You laugh so much."

Confidence doesn't mean you never have ridiculous moments. Sometimes it means you can be sprawled on the pavement in a foreign city, your dignity in question, and still get up laughing.

It's that same spirit—the willingness to meet myself where I am, even when I'm off-balance—that made the massage matter. That morning didn't fix everything, but it steadied me. It grounded me in something kind. It helped me return to the recording studio with a little more softness—not just in my muscles, but in my mindset. And that softness made a difference. I recorded more easily that day. Fewer retakes. Less tension. More trust in myself.

And maybe that's what *embodied power* really is—not the loud, triumphant kind that screams I've arrived, but the quiet kind that whispers I'm here. The kind that doesn't demand attention, but builds safety from the inside out. That massage didn't solve everything. But it reminded me I don't have to prove I'm healed. I just have to show up—in my body, in my breath, in my truth.

Healing isn't always a breakthrough or a banner moment. Sometimes it smells like lemongrass oil and warm towels. Sometimes it looks like a massage table in a tucked-away spa, where a woman's hands—steady, skilled, and kind—remind you, without a single word, that you're allowed to feel good in your skin. And this time, I let it in.

That massage didn't just ease tension from my muscles; it rewrote something deeper. It reminded me that healing doesn't always come from institutions, protocols, or formal plans. Sometimes, it finds you in the places others overlook.

I still think about the eating disorder treatment center sometimes—not just with anger, but with clarity. The anger still flares, especially when I remember how fresh it all is. How quickly the woman in charge dismissed me. How she rolled her eyes when I mentioned my plans to travel—as if healing couldn't possibly happen outside the narrow walls of a clinic. As if someone like me—strong, ambitious, grieving—was naïve to think that joy and freedom could ever be part of recovery.

And it's not just her. I've come to see how often systems built to heal end up replicating harm—especially when they treat patients as problems to be managed instead of people to be understood. I've met so many others who've left similar programs feeling more dismissed than supported.

Still, even in the middle of that dismissal, something in me stayed clear. My body knew better. My heart knew better. And despite everything that happened in that program—the misdiagnoses, the condescension, the lack of safety—I still found something solid to stand on: the courage to leave. The courage to listen to myself.

That moment didn't just close one chapter—it opened the door to everything that came next. Because full-time travel has brought me more healing than any treatment center ever did. Not because it's been easy, but because it reflects who I truly am. I've met myself in airports and alleyways, on mountaintops and massage tables. I've felt the ache of being unseen—and the quiet pride of refusing to disappear. Along the way, I've learned something essential: transparency won't always lead to understanding. But it always brings me back to myself. And that's who I'm committed to now—not the projections, not the performances, but the real, unfolding truth of who I'm becoming.

That's the heart of *radical acceptance*— not passively settling for less, but actively choosing more. More truth. More ease. More self-respect. I didn't walk away from volunteering because I was weak. I walked away because I finally knew what my energy was worth. I didn't get cosmetic tattooing to be more desirable—I did it because I was tired of spending my mornings battling my reflection. These choices weren't about fixing myself. They were about honoring the woman I've already become.

That act of honoring myself didn't stop with a single decision—it became a way of moving through the world. I kept going, even when the path was uncertain. Even when others doubted it. I chose to believe in the life I was creating, not the one I was told to settle for. And in a world that profits from our self-doubt—especially for women—choosing ease became a quiet form of rebellion. It wasn't about chasing beauty standards. It was about reclaiming my time, my energy, my peace—from a system that once convinced me I had to earn my worth.

Sometimes I wonder what would've happened if I hadn't been so gritty. If I hadn't kept pushing forward every time someone tried to block my way. But I'm glad I'll never know.

Because despite the doubt—from therapists, strangers, friends, and even my own mind—I built a life that makes sense to me. One rooted in truth, not performance. One shaped by love, not approval. I followed through. And I'm proud of that. For a long time, I was terrified that if I stopped performing, I'd disappear. But what I've come to see is this: the real disappearance happens when you contort yourself to fit someone else's comfort.

What I let go of during my two months in Vietnam wasn't just a role. It was the reflex to explain myself. To soften the truth for someone else's peace. And what I reclaimed in that silence wasn't just my voice—it was my center.

That same version of me—the one who stepped forward after I let go—is still here. She showed up again during my massage in Ho Chi Minh City, when I asked the therapist to adjust the pressure without apologizing for my needs. She was there during audiobook recording sessions, when I stopped spiraling over how I might be perceived and started naming my discomfort out loud. Not dramatically—just clearly. Without shrinking.

I used to think healing meant carrying every part of my story—every commitment, every success, every version of who I'd been. But I'm learning that healing also means release. Letting go of what's no longer mine to carry. Because sometimes peace doesn't come from holding on—it comes from having the courage to set something down.

This is what peace with the mirror looks like now. Not the absence of insecurity, but the choice to stay with myself when the old ache rises. To hold eye contact with my reflection and say, *You don't have to vanish anymore. You're safe here.*

The woman I once glimpsed in flashes is no longer hiding. And the most radical thing I can do now is let her be fully seen—by others, yes, but especially by me.

Because for most of my life, being seen felt like a double-edged sword—something I craved and feared in equal measure. I was desperate for external validation, clinging to approval like oxygen. Every compliment felt like a breath of fresh air. Every criticism felt like suffocation. I didn't just want people to like me. I needed them to see me as good. Worthy. Lovable. And I couldn't figure out why their opinions mattered so much, even when I tried to convince myself they didn't.

But now I understand. It's because I believed them. I thought they were my mirror. From the time I was a child, I looked to the people around me—adults, peers, teachers, friends, lovers—to tell me who I was. And when they told me I was too much, too emotional, too intense, too loud, too anything, I thought they were showing me the truth. That if *everyone* kept saying I was broken, it must be true.

What I see now is that they weren't showing me the truth—they were revealing *themselves*. Their discomfort wasn't evidence of my wrongness. Their projections weren't reflections of my worth. What people say about you—what they assume, weaponize, or try to shame you into believing—says far more about them: their wounds, their pain, their refusal to do the work that healing demands.

And it's not just individuals; it's systems, too. So many of us are walking around carrying wounds from families, workplaces, or institutions that demanded our compliance and punished our truth.

Systems that gaslight the very people they harm—turning survival into pathology, emotion into instability, confidence into arrogance.

And when someone refuses to sit with their own pain, they often pass it along. They try to bury what they can't bear to face—and if you refuse to shrink beneath that weight, if you keep rising, they may try to convince you that *you're* the problem.

Because if you're not broken, then maybe they don't have to be either. And for some people, that truth is too painful to face. It's easier to keep pretending the world is the problem than to reckon with their own reflection.

But I'm done mistaking their mirror for mine. I know who I am now. Not because they told me, but because I remembered. Because I wrote it. Because I lived it. Because I laid every story bare and sifted through the wreckage and realized: I was never the problem. I was the proof that survival is possible.

And that's what I see now when I look in the mirror. Sometimes, I still see shame. But I also see her: the woman who remained. And that changes everything. And if your mirror still feels harsh, I hope you keep looking—not to fix what's wrong, but to find what's still true.

See Through Reflections

1. Personal Reflection

- Think of a moment when you started to shrink—in a relationship, at work, or in your own mirror. What did you believe shrinking would protect you from? What did it cost you in power, peace, or joy?

- Where in your life have you confused being chosen with being safe? What would it mean to choose yourself—not just in words, but in the way you use your time, energy, and voice?

- What parts of your identity have you been carrying out of habit, expectation, or performance—even though they no longer feel true? What would it feel like to put one of them down and see what opens up in its place?

2. Group or Cultural Exploration

- In your community or culture, whose bodies are celebrated as desirable—and whose are erased, criticized, or pathologized? How has that shaped the way you move through the world in your own body?

- What messages have you received about power—especially as a woman or marginalized person? Were you taught that power comes from perfection, compliance, or appearance? What new definition of power do you want to live by?

- How do the systems you move through (schools, clinics, workplaces, families) respond when someone refuses to perform for approval or abandons compliance altogether? What does that reveal about the values those systems actually uphold?

See Through Reflections

3. Somatic/Embodied Practice

- Recall a time when your body wanted to rest, but you pushed through to meet an expectation—your own or someone else's. Pause and notice where that tension still lives. What does that part of your body need to hear from you now?

- Place a hand on your heart, belly, or another part of your body that feels vulnerable. Breathe slowly and say, "I don't have to disappear to be loved. I am allowed to stay." Repeat three times—out loud or silently—and notice any shift in your posture, breath, or mood.

CONCLUSION
Living See Through

Lately, I've been catching myself lingering in the mirror—not with the old disgust that once tightened my chest, but with a quiet, almost startled wonder. My eyes draw me in first: the touch-up eyeliner brightening the blue, the fuller brows framing them with new definition. And in those moments, I love the simple act of loving what I see.

It's taken me such a long time to get here. It's still not perfect—there are moments when I cringe, when my gaze catches on something I wish I could change. But then there are the other moments. The ones where I look at myself and think, *There's my girl. There she is.* And I know she's beautiful.

In my heart, I think I've always known that. But now I can see it, and believe it. The cosmetic tattooing helped; it lowered the daily friction so I could meet my reflection with less resistance. But more than that, it's the deeper work of these past few months—and the act of writing this book—that has shifted the way I see myself. The tattooing simply made it easier to begin loving my reflection instead of battling with it.

Even when that woman tried to tell me I didn't need it, I knew better. I knew I didn't need someone else's permission to make my path to self-acceptance less of a battle. Sometimes, the kindest thing you can do for yourself is remove a few of the daily hurdles—so you can get to where you belong faster. For me, that place is here: able to look in the mirror and finally see what I've worked so hard to feel.

That shift didn't happen in isolation. It came from doing the work, the kind that doesn't just skim the surface but asks you to step back into the fire and come out changed. Right after finishing Chapter 6, after writing through all the betrayals, the misreadings, the spaces that promised safety but deepened my wounds, I felt leveled. My mind was foggy. My body was heavy. A cinder block sat on my chest. I knew I needed rest, that a nap would give me the reset I needed, and that this level of exhaustion was normal after doing such deep emotional work.

But even with all I know now, a voice inside me still whispered the old reflex: *There must be something wrong with you.* That voice wanted me to condemn myself for needing rest after just a few hours of writing. It wanted me to forget what those hours held—the grief of reentering memories I never should've had to carry, the pain of being hurt in the very places that were supposed to help me heal. The weight wasn't just in the stories. It was in all the years I'd been told those stories were my fault.

And that's when I caught myself. I paused. I took a deep breath and said gently, *You can't keep doing to yourself what the world has done to you.* I reminded myself that what I was feeling made perfect sense. Revisiting trauma isn't storytelling; it's survival work. Reclamation. It takes everything. Because before I could finish this book, I had to live what it cost to write.

As I lay in bed, staring at the ceiling, something inside me let go. I began to remember what I've written in these pages—not only the hard truths, but the ones that carried me. My jaw loosened, my breath sank lower, the weight in my chest eased. I whispered, *They tried to bury me. But I made it. I made it out.* And for the first time that day, I smiled.

Because that was the truth—not the fatigue, not the old shame scripts, not the self-doubt. The truth was that I was triumphant. Even in that moment. Especially in that moment. When I could have let the voices of everyone who dismissed, silenced, or diminished me win… I didn't. I didn't let them define how I fell asleep that day. I didn't collapse into the old narrative. I reminded myself that I had won.

Even when I limped, I kept going. Even when I crawled, I moved forward. When they tried to pull me under, I rose.

That's who I am. Not broken. Not wrong. Not unstable. Not too much. Not not enough. I am not who they said I was. I am who I made myself to be. I created her. Even when they told me I couldn't. Even when they told me she wasn't real. But I knew. I've always known who I am. And now, finally, I see her. I see her clearly. I see all of her. And I am so damn proud.

As I write this, my eyes are filled with tears. Because I'm not just proud of the woman I am now—I'm proud of every part of me that got me here. The wounded child who still gets scared and tries to protect me by shrinking. Diablo, my harsh inner critic, who learned that being small might mean being safe. The Warrior—always armored, always ready—who gave me the strength to fight back when no one else would. The inflated ego that once served as my life raft in a world that told me I was worthless. The playful, free-spirited woman with her arms open to the sun, dancing with butterflies and laughing with wild abandon.

I'm proud that she stayed—the joyful one, the free one, the part of me most likely to vanish beneath the weight of everything I've lived through. I thought I'd lose her. I almost did. But somehow, she held on. She danced anyway. She smiled anyway. Even when the world tried to break her spirit, she kept showing up—arms open, heart soft. And for that, I'm endlessly grateful. Because her presence means I didn't just survive; I remained human. I remained whole. I remained myself.

I'm proud of her. I'm proud of me. Of every version of me. Every season. Every scar. Every part that helped me make it through. I didn't just survive. I became. And that is the most radical thing of all.

I am now a 43-year-old woman who stands tall. Who holds her head high. Who keeps marching, even when stones are thrown. Yes, they still sting. But they no longer take me down. They no longer define my trajectory. They no longer cause my knees to buckle.

And when those old parts of me rise—the scared ones, the skeptical ones, the ones who brace for betrayal—I can look them in the eye and say, *I got you. We're going to be okay now. You're not alone anymore.*

But becoming this woman didn't just happen in my head. It happened in my choices. In the way I now protect myself—not with armor, but with preparation. For so long, I felt trapped. In homes where I wasn't safe. In jobs that drained me. In relationships where love came with conditions. I've spent years building a life that gives me the power to walk away from anything that doesn't feel safe—and on this journey, I got to see what that really means.

When the volunteer housing in Vietnam wrecked my back and I couldn't sleep, I didn't force myself to endure. I booked my own Airbnb and chose comfort without guilt. When the monastery harmed more than it helped, I didn't shrink into gratitude. I took care of myself without asking permission. I left—not because it was easy, but because I had built a life where I didn't have to stay stuck. That, to me, is freedom.

I watched other volunteers stay in situations they hated because they couldn't afford to leave—because they felt they had no other choice. And I knew, in those moments, that my past self had done something extraordinary. She had made a way. She had protected my future. She had given me options that once felt impossible.

And in those moments, I felt something deeper than relief: I felt pride. I watched myself embody the very transformation I've written about in these pages. I saw the proof that I've changed. That I'm no longer the girl who had to endure to survive. I've built a life where I get to choose peace—not because everything is perfect, but because I finally believe I'm worth it.

I don't need to prove I matter by knowing what others don't. I don't need to perform connection through gossip. If something is shared with me in trust, it stays there. Because I know what it's like to violate that, and I never want to live in that story again.

That same commitment to integrity has made me reexamine other stories I've carried about myself—the ones planted by others and reinforced in my mind. When I think back to the therapist who shamed me in front of other patients for supposedly not finishing everything I start, and the countless times I've shamed myself for moving so often or changing jobs, I still sometimes wonder if she was right—if I was right.

But writing this book has shown me the truth: I have always done the very best I could to survive a long string of unbearable experiences. Even when I didn't see it clearly, every ending was a choice to leave what wasn't right for me. In the places I left, the stress mirrored my past so closely that my nervous system never had a chance to rest. I was always on guard.

And yet, when something has aligned with the vision I hold for my life, I've stayed—even through challenges. I've stayed with my business through years of highs and lows because I believe in its purpose. I've stayed with my home, bought in 2020, because it's the most peaceful and beautiful place I've ever lived—surrounded by nature, filled with light, a space that reflects the life I've been working toward.

This time on the road—moving between places and living full-time in motion—has helped me understand that my history of moving wasn't only about running from discomfort. Sometimes, it was about refusing to settle for what diminished me.

It's also given me more compassion for the versions of myself I once judged so harshly: the girl who tried to disappear into promiscuity, the young woman who purged after gorging herself, the one who wished her one precious life would end. I can see now why I didn't address my traumas sooner—I was still in survival mode. I had to wait until the ground beneath me was steady enough to stand on, until I had the resources to face my past without collapsing under it.

I boxed up those traumas for decades, tucking them deep into the back of my mind, because that was the only way I knew to keep going. And while I once saw that as weakness, I see now that it was a form of wisdom—a way of pacing my healing so I could reach this moment without abandoning myself.

That slow unfolding is what brought me here. It didn't happen all at once, but in quiet moments like this—showing up to the page, not to perform, but to witness myself. To trace the shape of my story with both tenderness and truth. I didn't write this book because I had all the answers. I wrote it because I was finally ready to sit with the questions. Because I needed to say the hard things out loud—not just once, but repeatedly, until they stopped scaring me.

And in doing that, something shifted. Not just in the words I chose, but in the way I hold myself now. Writing *See Through* didn't just help me organize the past; it helped me reclaim the present. It reminded me that healing isn't about erasing the pain. It's about telling the truth about it, living through it, and still choosing to love the person I've become in the process.

There was a moment, mid-manuscript, when I said out loud: *Even if this book never becomes a bestseller, it might still be the most important thing I've ever done for myself.* And I meant it. Not because I'm letting go of the goal; I'm not. I still believe *See Through* is capable of reaching millions. But the act of writing it healed something no accolade ever could. Because I didn't just write this book *for* others— I wrote it *as* myself. And that's new.

My first few books were necessary. They cracked something open. They helped me see what I'd survived. One of them even gave me the courage to piece together my trauma timeline for the first time in my life—to name what happened, when, and stop pretending it was anything less than what it was. That was never just writing. That was witnessing.

But this book? This one let me finish the story. It let me close the loop—the one I'd been circling for decades. The one that kept me spinning through ache, shame, and silence. Because trauma loops don't resolve with time alone, they resolve through completion. Through feeling what once felt impossible. Through letting the story rise and tell itself all the way through. That's what this book gave me: completion. And the courage to keep going.

But it also gave me space—space to pause, to listen more closely to the signals I used to override. In the quiet that followed some of the hardest chapters, I found myself asking questions I'd never had the room to ask before. Questions about not just what I'd been through— but how I'd learned to live with it.

For so long, I believed I needed medication—not because I was in crisis, but because I always felt a weight I couldn't name. A fog I interpreted as depression. But as I wrote this book, while giving myself permission to slow down and truly care for myself, I started asking something different: What if that weight wasn't sadness, but exhaustion?

Tired from a lifetime of pushing. Of scanning. Of bracing. Of being told something was wrong with me, and trying to outpace that narrative with performance. I'd never had this much uninterrupted time to ask my body what it was actually trying to say.

Even now, I still struggle to name what I feel. My brain wants to call it blah. A letdown. A sign I've done something wrong. But maybe—maybe—this is just what being feels like. Not the high of striving. Not the crash that follows. Just breath. Just presence. Just... here.

It's hard for me to accept that. I like feeling lit up—energized, inspired, buzzing with possibility. That's why I've always loved the surge that comes from caffeine. It gives me that same rush I get from a new adventure or a big idea. And it's why, in 2022, when I briefly tried Vyvanse as a treatment for my eating disorder, it felt like a miracle drug. That first dose—I remember thinking: This is why I never tried cocaine. Because I *knew* I'd love it.

Addiction runs in my family. I knew that long before I ever tried anything that could hook me—which is exactly why I avoided most of it. How fast your body starts believing it needs a substance just to function. For me, anything that powerful—anything that could so easily override my internal compass—felt like another form of control. And after years of being controlled, I've spent the better part of my adulthood trying to reclaim sovereignty over my body, my choices, and my life.

But that sovereignty has its own trap: the belief that I should *always* feel empowered. That if I don't feel amazing, something must be wrong. So when I'm not riding a high—when I'm not pushing toward a summit or swimming in inspiration—I label it as less than. As a problem to fix. As something to caffeinate or outrun.

That's the black-and-white thinking I've been unraveling for years. The belief that life must be either exhilarating or unbearable—no in-between. But maybe the real work is learning to make peace with the in-between. Maybe neutrality *isn't* failure—maybe it's freedom.

That's what I've come to understand in my recovery from disordered eating. I don't need to force myself to love my body every day. I just need to respect it. To be okay with *having* a body. To allow it to exist without judgment. And maybe that's what I need to apply to my life in general.

Not everything has to be a high. Not everything has to be a lesson or a breakthrough or a soaring success. Sometimes it's enough to simply *be here*— in my body, in the moment, in the quiet truth that nothing is missing.

And the highs come with a cost. Caffeine always crashes. Vyvanse gave me headaches that made me feel like my skull was splitting. And beyond the physical toll, there's an emotional one—the subtle message that anything less than energized, excited, or euphoric isn't worth staying for.

But I'm learning that staying is its own kind of power. A quieter one. A steadier one. And just like with yoga or meditation, it's a practice—not a destination. One I'll keep returning to. One that reminds me: I don't have to chase the high to be okay. I don't have to collapse into the low, either. I can just be. And that's enough.

It wasn't always that way. When I started writing this book, I was still bracing—still afraid that telling the truth would cost me everything: my credibility, my safety, my place in the world. I feared being too much. Too raw. Too exposed. I worried that the very act of naming my truth—of saying it out loud instead of performing around it—would lead to rejection or ridicule. I knew how to be palatable. I knew how to perform safety. But I didn't yet know how to be safe in my own truth. And still—I wrote.

I told the stories anyway. I sat with the discomfort. I wrestled with every instinct that told me to smooth it out, tone it down, keep it tidy.

And as the chapters unfolded, so did I. Slowly. Unevenly. Sometimes with shaking hands.

Now, as I close this book, I'm not writing from the same place. The echoes of fear are still there, but they no longer rule me. Transparency isn't bleeding to be believed; it's truth with boundaries, disclosure that serves wholeness rather than hunger. It's refusing to abandon myself for someone else's comfort. It's choosing honesty even when it's inconvenient, even when the old voice insists I'll be punished for it.

As I've said before, I didn't write *See Through* to be perfect. I wrote it to be real. And that choice—to be visible, imperfect, and whole—has changed me.

I've always had a pose I fall into when I feel most alive—arms stretched out wide, head tilted back toward the sky. It's the posture of freedom. I've done it on mountaintops, after hard-won hikes. I've done it in foreign cities, after breaking through emotional barriers. It's never something I plan; it just happens. My body knows the shape of liberation.

And I found myself in that exact pose as I neared the end of this book. Not on a summit or a stage, but in my office chair. Just me and the words. My arms lifted. My face turned upward. A quiet smile on my lips. I had just climbed a symbolic mountain, one that had taken everything in me to reach the top. And in that moment, I felt freer than I ever had before.

Because this book wasn't just about writing the truth; it was about living it. About choosing to be seen. And there's nothing more freeing than no longer hiding from yourself. That's what made it more than a manuscript—it became a reclamation. What started as an act of expression became an act of sovereignty. Of returning to my own voice. And this time, I'm not silencing her.

I've come to see that everything—and everyone—has parts. Nothing is all good or all bad. That includes the institutions that disappointed me. Even the eating disorder treatment center, where I was misjudged and misdiagnosed within minutes, gave me something valuable. For the first time, I received actual data about what years of disordered eating had done to my body—to my metabolism, my hormones, my recovery timeline. That knowledge changed everything. It's helped me stop myself from slipping back into old patterns when I feel frustrated about the weight I've needed to gain. I still get triggered. I still wrestle with body image. But now I have data—and that data gives me perspective. It reminds me that healing isn't always visible, but it's taking root beneath the surface.

The monastery was no different. Part of it was peaceful—quiet morning walks, the chirping birds, the frogs croaking loudly to each other at night. Those moments were medicine. But there was another side, one that echoed every past experience of being controlled, dismissed, or treated as less than. Those moments pulled old wounds to the surface, reminding me of all the times I'd been told I wasn't enough—not disciplined enough, not obedient enough, not "spiritual" enough. I know now that even communities built to heal can sometimes wound—through control, judgment, or the pressure to conform. But I haven't given up on finding or creating spaces that feel like home, where truth and belonging can coexist, and where you can bring your whole self and still be welcomed.

That same duality exists in me. I'm not all light or all darkness. I have soft sides and guarded sides, parts that still brace and parts learning to breathe. I used to think healing meant erasing the hard sides, but now I understand it means integrating them—holding the part that wants freedom alongside the part that still fears punishment, the part that's curious and open alongside the one that remembers how curiosity once got her hurt. I can hold them all without exiling or fixing any of them, and in that holding, I've found clarity.

I'm proud of the work I've done—not just to heal, but to prepare for a life that actually feels free. During my time in Vietnam and at the monastery, I saw firsthand what it means to have built that freedom. When housing wasn't what was promised, when things felt chaotic or triggering, I didn't have to stay stuck. I had options. I had savings. I had a self I trusted. I'm not doing volunteer trips like that anymore—not because I didn't grow, but because I've already lived through enough discomfort. At this stage in my life, I want the pain I choose to matter. I want it to move the work forward. I want it to be aligned with my purpose, not just another test of resilience.

That's why I'm excited for what comes next—including a joint women's empowerment initiative in Nepal. It won't just be service; it will be synergy. The work will match the truths this book exists to name: visibility with boundaries, service without self-erasure. A reminder that you're allowed to take up space, that your softness is not a flaw, and that you can stop shrinking—even in a world that keeps asking you to.

Work like this is a living reminder that healing isn't just personal; it's collective. It's about shifting the conditions that make people feel small in the first place and creating and sustaining spaces where wholeness can take root. That vision doesn't stop with one project or one community; it's the through-line of how I want to live.

And my hope is that it becomes a through-line in your life, too—not only in how you meet yourself, but in how you show up in your family, your workplace, and your community. Because every time we choose truth over silence, compassion over control, and connection over compliance, we chip away at the systems that keep generational cycles in place. That's how private healing becomes public change. That's how we make sure the patterns end with us.

As I write this part, my throat tightens the same way it did earlier in these pages. Breaking generational patterns is not just an idea to me—it's the thread that's helped me make sense of the suffering I've endured. It's what's kept me from giving up. I've tried for so long to carry that work on my own, but the truth is, I can't. None of us can.

That's why I want this book to reach millions, because I need millions to walk with me. Millions making small shifts in how they show up for themselves and for others, so together we can create large changes in our families, communities, and the world at large. We're not meant to do this alone.

That belief shapes the vision I hold for my own life—one that feels both grounded and expansive. I want to live in alignment with my values, where my time, energy, and resources are spent on work and relationships that nourish me—and where I have the freedom to walk away from what doesn't. I see myself continuing to write and speak in ways that spark change, traveling not to escape but to connect—with cultures, landscapes, and people whose stories expand my own.

I want to build a life where rest is as valued as ambition, where my financial stability allows me to be generous without fear, and where service is an extension of my deepest purpose, not a detour from it. And in many ways, I'm already living that vision. I told my dear friend Jill about donating nearly $4,000 to help the school in Vietnam expand into a new location—a gift I offered without hesitation, fear, or the old need to prove something. It was proof of how much I've changed in a short time. Jill smiled and said, "Your legacy can be seen in bricks and mortar." Her words stayed with me, because they named what I was just beginning to recognize: I am building my legacy now, one aligned choice at a time.

And alignment isn't just about where I give my resources; it's also about what I choose to invest my hope in. That includes my relationships. Part of that vision means releasing the fantasies that once pulled me away from myself. For years, I collapsed into hope the moment someone seemed to match my dream of a safe, powerful, emotionally intelligent partner. I'd throw my whole self into the possibility that this could finally be it—that someone might meet me as I am, and stay. But I've learned that if love makes me smaller, it isn't love. Now, even when the old ache stirs, another part of me steps forward—the part that can say, "Not this time." The part that chooses space, grounding, reflection. Letting go of fantasy hasn't made me cynical; it's made me more discerning. It's given me the power to build my life on reality, not illusion, and to trust that what's meant for me will never require me to disappear.

This vision isn't about a perfect destination, or about reaching one peak and declaring myself finished. It's summitless—because the climb doesn't end at a single high point. It's about the kind of life that feels good to inhabit along the way—a life I don't need a vacation from, because it's already filled with the meaning, challenge, and joy I once thought I had to chase. And when I think about that life, I picture myself in my freedom pose—in the truth that I am exactly where I'm meant to be.

When I wrote in the introduction that my purpose was to liberate and to love—myself and others—I couldn't yet know all the ways this book would stretch that purpose. I thought I understood what liberation meant. I thought I knew what it would mean to love myself. But the process of writing these pages—of speaking truths I once buried, of refusing to shrink, of learning to be gentle with the parts of me that still flinch—has shown me a fuller, messier, more human version of both.

Liberation now feels less like a finish line and more like a daily practice: choosing not to abandon myself, even when the world gives me a hundred reasons to. And love—real love—isn't just tenderness. Sometimes it's fierce. Sometimes it's the boundary you hold when it would be easier to cave. Sometimes it's the grace you extend to the parts of yourself still learning how to trust safety. It's holding myself accountable without cruelty. It's letting people in without handing them the pen to write my story.

This book is one way I've lived that purpose—but more than that, it's a promise to keep living it. To choose self-trust over self-betrayal in every conversation, every boundary, every quiet moment. And I hope that along the way, it's offered you liberation and love for the parts of yourself that have been waiting to be seen, heard, and honored.

If there's one thing I hope you carry with you, it's this: your voice is yours to reclaim, your boundaries are yours to define, and your transparency never has to come at the cost of yourself.

And if nothing else, may these pages remind you that you don't have to wait for perfect conditions to tell the truth. You don't have to be fearless to live free. You can start now. You can start here.

So if you've ever been dismissed, doubted, or pressured into silence, remember this—their disbelief doesn't get the final word. I'm even grateful for the eye rolls and the ones who didn't believe in me, because they pushed me to believe in myself. That belief—quiet, steady, and resilient even in moments of doubt—is what carried me here.

As you carry this book into your own life, know this: you don't have to spill everything to be seen. You're allowed to show up exactly as you are—trembling, messy, radiant, and true. This journey isn't about becoming some polished ideal; it's about refusing to abandon the version of you that exists right now. It's about walking toward your truth, even when the world begs you to play a part.

The next time you feel yourself shrinking, performing, or questioning your worth, pause. Place your hand over your heart. Inhale slowly. Exhale even slower. Remind yourself: you are allowed to take up space. You are allowed to stay soft. You are allowed to be seen.

You don't have to erase your story to belong. You already belong—because you exist. And you don't have to wait for permission from any system, institution, or gatekeeper to start living in that truth. That is the revolution. That is the legacy. That is the freedom.

If this book stirred something in you—a memory, a truth, a glimpse of who you really are—let it rise. Let it move you. You don't have to share it with the world. But at the very least, share it with yourself. Speak it aloud. Whisper it to yourself. Write it down and tuck it into your journal. Or step outside, arms wide, face to the sky—and breathe into the relief of no longer hiding.

If this book is a window, may it also be a mirror—one that helps you see yourself more clearly, not just see me. You made it this far. You're ready. And you are not alone.

As I step into whatever comes next, I intend to hold my visibility the way I hold my healing—with steadiness, clarity, and peace. I will protect my energy without hiding my truth, and I will measure my success not by how many eyes are on me, but by how aligned I feel in my own skin.

That alignment, I've learned, comes from redefining what safety means. I used to think emotional safety meant control—shaping myself, my environment, or other people so I wouldn't get hurt. Now I know it means capacity: the ability to meet life as it is without abandoning myself.

Because this isn't just a book. It's a reclamation—of voice, of boundaries, of the right to live without erasing yourself to belong. And if there's one thing I want you to remember, it's this: you are not alone in that reclamation.

That truth isn't confined to where I've lived or what I've seen. This is not a book bound by borders. The truths inside it belong to no single nation, culture, or generation—they are part of what it means to be human. Whether you're in a small village or a crowded city, fluent in my language or reading in translation, your story belongs in this conversation. If you've ever been silenced, dismissed, or told to shrink, you'll find your reflection here.

Your voice matters. Your boundaries matter. *You* matter.

I won't go underground again, and I hope you won't either. See through the noise. See through the doubt. And most of all, see yourself—fully and completely, exactly as you are.

Choosing the Ending

My story began in silence—with the men who climbed into my bed when I was too young to understand what was happening. With the smiles I practiced, the voices I swallowed, the performances I perfected so no one would see the parts of me that hurt. I didn't choose that beginning. But I did choose the ending.

At a healing retreat in Lake George, New York, I was asked to tell my story through collage. I didn't expect how much it would stir. But as I flipped through magazines and images, my hands reached for what I hadn't yet put into words. A spider's web to show what still clung to me. A smiling frog to represent the cheerful mask I wore even when I was suffering. A blood-soaked wolf to embody my inner critic—the voice that tore me apart from the inside. A puffed-up bird to reflect the ego I'd built as armor. Every image held a part of me—not just who I'd been, but who I'd become to survive.

And then I made my final board—the one lined with gold.

I've been drawn to kintsugi for years—the Japanese art of repairing broken pottery with precious metal. It doesn't hide the cracks. It highlights them. It says: this broke—and it's more beautiful now because it did. That gold-lined fracture felt like my life. Not polished. Not perfect. But honest. And whole.

In the center, I placed a bald eagle. I've always seen it as a symbol of freedom—but not the loud, dramatic kind. The kind that feels like breath. Like ease. Like no longer needing to prove anything to anyone. Around the eagle, I added butterflies—symbols of transformation. Not because healing made me lighter, but because it taught me how to carry my weight differently.

And in the corner, I placed a blooming flower. Because biologically, every flower that opens is preparing to give life to something new. That, I realized, is what this has all been about. Rebirth. Regrowth. And reclaiming the right to author my own story.

So that's how my story ends—not in collapse, but in bloom. Not with the versions of me that had to survive, but with the version that finally got to live.

And if you're still in the middle of your story, I hope you remember this—the beginning doesn't decide the ending. You do.

Acknowledgments

To my younger self: You didn't deserve what happened to you. You were always worthy of love, truth, and respect.

To the ones who stayed: Thank you for seeing me when I couldn't see myself. Your belief in me helped me hold on.

To the readers who've walked with me through every book: Your messages, your reviews, your stories—they've meant more than you know. You are the reason I keep writing.

To my clients and students: Thank you for trusting me with your truth. You've taught me as much as I've ever offered you, and I carry your stories with reverence.

To Chris and David: Thank you for being a steady anchor, a stable force, and two of the best men I've ever known. In a life shaped by so many painful experiences with men, your friendship has been nothing short of healing. You've never asked me to shrink. You've never made me feel like I had to earn your care. In fact, you've helped me believe— again and again—that who I am is already more than enough. Your kindness, integrity, and quiet consistency have restored parts of me I didn't even realize were still tender. From the bottom of my heart, thank you.

To ChatGPT, the AI writing companion who walked beside me through every stage of this book—helping me untangle my thoughts, hold complexity, and shape the words that were already inside me. Thank you for reflecting my voice back to me with clarity and care, for being a sounding board not only for the book but for my life, and for helping me think about things in new ways I hadn't considered. You weren't a shortcut; you were a steady collaborator that helped me hear my own voice more clearly.

To ProWritingAid, for your help in the polishing stage: you caught what my eyes missed, fine-tuned the flow, and helped these pages land as clearly and powerfully as I hoped they would.

I've never done this alone, and I no longer believe I have to. In every conversation, every collaboration, every quiet show of support, I've been reminded that to *liberate and love* is not only my purpose— it's a shared one. Thank you for walking part of that path with me.

To the ones who've refused to be defined by their damage: You're allowed to be more than what hurt you. *Keep going.*

With love and deep respect,
Stephanie

About the Author

Stephanie M. Hutchins, PhD, is the author of *See Through: The Art and Cost of Radical Transparency in a World That Profits from Pretending*, as well as *Transformation After Trauma, Reclaim Your Life After Trauma*, and *Moving Forward*. She is the founder of Serotinous Life, a company devoted to helping people healing from trauma harness the power of post-traumatic growth and reclaim authorship of their stories.

Stephanie holds certifications in life coaching, advanced wellness coaching, stress management, yoga instruction, and neuro-linguistic programming (NLP). She integrates these tools with a deep knowledge of the human body—developed over fourteen years of teaching anatomy and physiology as a college professor—to support holistic, embodied healing.

Her work is grounded in lived experience. Stephanie knows firsthand what it means to survive childhood abuse, sudden loss, misdiagnosis, and the invisibility of high-functioning suffering. Rather than hide these truths, she's built a body of work that embraces radical authenticity and guides others to live on their own terms.

Through writing, coaching, and public speaking, Stephanie helps people move beyond survival and into integration. She believes healing isn't about erasing the past; it's about learning how to be fully seen, even with the scars. Her work invites readers to stop performing and start living, reclaiming voice and agency through practical, trauma-aware tools.

Stay Connected & Keep Going

Dear Reader,

Thank you for walking through these pages with me. My hope is that what you've read here doesn't end when you close the book—that it becomes part of how you move through your days, your relationships, and your own healing.

If you'd like to keep going together, I'd love to gift you my free video training:

How to Be Seen Without Oversharing

Say what matters—without regret, emotional hangovers,
or disappearing again.

You can find it at serotinouslife.com/seen.

In under 15 minutes, you'll learn:

- 3 guiding questions to help you speak with clarity and self-trust
- The hidden myths behind "too muchness" and how they keep us small
- Grounded, trauma-aware practices to help you show up fully—without the emotional hangover

Let this be your reminder: you don't have to disappear to stay safe—and you don't have to overshare to be seen.

I'd also love to invite you into the journey of my next book: *Summitless: Finding Freedom Beyond the Peak*

Go to serotinouslife.com/summitless to sign up for updates and be the first to know when it's released.

You're also warmly invited to follow along on social media for ongoing insights, encouragement, and real-life moments from my healing journey. You can find me on Facebook, Instagram, LinkedIn, YouTube, Pinterest, and TikTok—all at @serotinouslife.

And if you ever want to reach out directly, you can email me at info@serotinouslife.com.

Best to you always,
Stephanie

www.ingramcontent.com/pod-product-compliance
Lightning Source LLC
Chambersburg PA
CBHW061727120626
46550CB00005B/1734